un\ \martyred

un\ \martyred:
[self-]vanishing presences
in Vietnamese poetry

Nhã Thuyên

ROOF BOOKS
NEW YORK

Copyright © 2019 Nhã Thuyên
ISBN: 978-1-931824-81-1
Library of Congress Control Number: 2019931031

Book and cover design by Mabel Capability Taylor

Author drawing by Đinh Trường Chinh

Cover art © by Trần Trung Tín, *Mẹ cõng con (Mother carries son)*, 1973, oil on
newspaper, 54.5 x 38.5 cm. Private collection. With permission from Trần
Trung Tín's wife Trần Thị Huỳnh Nga.

This book is made possible, in part, by the New York State Council on the
Arts with the support of Governor Andrew Cuomo and the New York State
Legislature.

Roof Books
are published by
Segue Foundation
300 Bowery, New York, NY 10012
seguefoundation.com

Roof Books
are distributed by
Small Press Distribution
1341 Seventh Street
Berkeley, CA 94710-1403
800-869-7553 or spdbooks.org

for dialogues in dunes & dust,
resilient counterparts, muted bearings & need-to-come endings

Table of Contents

mỗi ngày, tôi nhai hết một màu xanh cọng cỏ & mười xác chết
nuốt sạch 30 ký điện mà vẫn còn thèm

each day, i chew up grassy green & ten dead bodies
devour 30 kilowatts of electricity and still crave for more.

— Phan Bá Thọ

Vâng, thể xác cô ấy là sự chuyển động.

Yes, her body is motion.

— Trần Minh Quân

Acknowledging the Encounters

I bear gratitude for the trustful support and patient companionship of presences namable and silent, what with the inevitable errata of memory.

I sincerely thank Arts Network Asia (www.artsnetworkasia.org) for their financial assistance with the Underground Voices project in early 2011. Thank you Institut français du Việt Nam (Hà Nội) for planning a discussion program on this project's poetic phenomena, although the scheduled talk on January 5, 2012 was eventually cancelled and did not have a chance to occur.

Thank you *Tia Sáng magazine* and Trung Nguyên Creative Space for allowing me to present a part of my research in the talk *A Vietnamese Contemporary Poetry Corner* on June 23, 2012.

Thank you Heinrich Böll Stiftung Southeast Asia for supporting me in the process of finalizing this book.

Thank you, editors of *Da Màu* magazine for publishing the early Vietnamese original versions of essays, interviews, and videos featuring the Mở Miệng (Open Mouth) group in late 2012. Thank you, the following editors and magazines that have offered space and editorial inputs for the essays' English translations, sometimes with a different title: *Nguyễn Quốc Chánh* on *Asymptote* (2015); *Womxn's Poetry: A Resonance of Voices in Vietnamese Poetry* on *Cordite Review* (2017); *Poetry of Negation and the Negation of Poetry* on *Full Stop* (2017); *[Un-]contextualizing Underground Poetry: Reimagining a Critical Community* on *Words Without Borders* (November, 2018); *Open Mouth: The Revolt of Trash* on *Jacket2* (2019). The essay *The Possibilities and Limits of Play: Poetry and [Self-]publishing Practices in Việt Nam Today* was previously published in the bilingual anthology of essays *We, Now, Here, There, Together | Chúng ta, lúc này, đây, đó, cùng nhau* (A-festival & AJAR Press, 2017). Other related research in this project has been presented in the conferences: *Southeast Asian Understanding of Freedom of Expression: Re-defining From the Ground*, organized by Foundation for Community Educational Media (FCEM) and Heinrich Böll Stiftung (HBS) SEA office

(Bangkok, November 2015) and the roundtable discussion on publishing at A-festival (Hà Nội, August 2016). Thank you, Rebecca Teich at Roof Books for enduringly reading and exchanging thoughts to make the transplanted book shared more as a whole in a different context.

From innermost depths, thank you translators, friends, readers, precious and intimate beings who have offered me refuge from the first moment of penning to the last edits of the essays, gifting me incalculable amounts of time and energy, carrying my utterances into another language: Kaitlin Rees, David Payne, Ngân Nguyễn, Nguyễn Hoàng Quyên, Hải Ngọc-Trần Ngọc Hiếu. I am enwrapped in their pure love of literature and unconditional affection for friends.

I would like to dedicate a special note of gratitude to Professor Nguyễn Thị Bình, who has openly embraced and welcomed my naïve recklessness since my college days. This book is thus my response to her patiently quiet longing for an open milieu of letters, and to my own supposedly mute passiveness for the past several years ever since she and I, in different manners, were suspended from our teaching jobs at the Literature Department, Hà Nội National University of Education.

I am debt-bound, emotionally, literarily, to friends here and elsewhere, beings whom I've met or passed by in meta-space, beings who have read me, gifted me encounters, opened me to other literatures, beings who have inched closer to one another to express multidirectional voices in the story between literature and politics—a story perhaps forever without a peaceful ending, beings who have struggled for and defended the existence of diverse literatures, beings who have together shared and negotiated the repercussions of literature. Not only is the formation of this book indebted to them, but I myself might have given up on the project had it not been for the conversations, jests or moments of sitting in silence together. For these innumerable presences, I hope to be a whispered gratitude.

My appreciation goes out to all the authors whose works and lives have warmly welcomed me in. After all, had it not been for the encounters with those who more or less had to suffer through the repercussions of their literary love and labor, my act of reading would never have started. I still see myself as the fortunate beneficiary of these encounters. This book, therefore, is dedicated to these enduring fellow sufferers, with a humble wish to return to the most useless place: a shared reading, an anonymous reading. I could only thank these generosities by lettered romances, by not giving up on the private and shared literary work whose presence often manifests as a distance, a silence, a lack, for a presence is also forever (demanding to be) an absence.

Hà Nội, December, 2018
Nhã Thuyên

From the Author
translated by David Payne

An attempt at conversation is always an attempt to reach a thorough understanding, meaning to unceasingly face misunderstandings. An attempt to search out traces and connections. An attempt to erase and to insert some question marks. An attempt to encounter those with shared illusions, shared struggles, shared understandings. An attempt to accept others outside and within oneself. As a result, while the conversation about poetry in this collection is a dialogue, it is also a monologue. I stumble over personal pronouns: at one moment saying "I," then at another preferring "I, plural."

Though I am named as the author, this is not the fruit of individual labor; like all reading, it yearns to be a reading *with*. Formed over seven years, or perhaps even longer, first my graduate thesis on the Mở Miệng (Open Mouth) group and then the *Underground Voices* project provided the basis for these essays (renewed many times over the period from approximately 2011 to 2018), I don't know how to name the strangers and companions, the ruptures and connections, the arrivals and departures that have gone along with me.

As I have been intensely preoccupied with the entanglements of Vietnamese poetry, and endeavoring to understand thoroughly the-things-that-occur around me, it is as if, over many long years, I keep getting stuck in those-things-that-were-past-but-continually-reoccur, with half-answered questions. Why these (Vietnamese) poets? The saboteurs, the protestors, the marginalized, the ones who don't belong? Why these presences seemingly forced to be absent? Fond of quietness, I found myself closer to anomalous utterances, to the faint of heart, to silenced voices, to those on the edge, to thicker, deeper, more silent shadows. I was, however, alarmed by the vehemence, the clamor, the derision. Of course, fighting is also not necessarily a Vietnamese specialty. The capacity to wordlessly endure a legacy of tears doesn't need to be multiplied forever. When a poetic language faces life or death, when language has to struggle and cry out to break free from its bonds, to give itself a chance to open up, then these poetic presences, to me, involve laborious and noteworthy choices. I force myself to stay and listen to these sounds, attempting to translate these hardships into the language of a reader. It isn't even a choice: I [plural] am unable to avoid joining myself with others and others with myself, am unable to avoid listening and offering words, if I expect to be a presence in this community, where the story of one individual (or many) is always (of necessity) a common story.

If I must have a message in these pages, I think it is that the attempt to write these [self-]vanishing presences into existence is also, for me, a critical reflection on the Vietnamese language. I do not seek a Vietnamese that rails angrily, a hot-headed Viet-namese, a Vietnamese that seeks to incite. Yet behind all the anger stirred up in the pages of these marginalized poets, I hear the story of a Vietnamese language that is mistreated, that is mistreating itself, and attempting to survive. Something else is alongside | shines through: a Vietnamese that is light, playful, and full of osmotic potential. A Vietnamese that doesn't shirk collisions and alterations as it attempts to protect its beauty and to nurture its potential. A Vietnamese that doesn't accept to be silenced. For this reason, I don't want the English trans-lation of this collection to be seen merely as an introduction to a Vietnamese literature that has never yet appeared in any national magazine or in literary diplomacy aimed at "foreign-ers," but rather, in an illusion of equality, I want Vietnamese language and literature to collide and be in dialogue with other languages, with other literatures. I am blind and disoriented: is there any real difference between the reader and the author, within and without, Vietnamese and non-Vietnamese? Where did I expect to find it? Here. There. In the original in the trans-lation. Would it create more possibilities for human touch?

Each writer in this story has repercussions that only seem to resonate with few: poetry and the possibilities of poetry sur-vive in its own language. Why do I [plural] still read and write poetry? Why do poetic utterances need to be heard, and understood? Can poetic words more or less engage me [plural] with a poetic way of living? Why do I have to display my writing and reading self? I read poems, I make poems visible, and poems read me, and make me visible. My reading is a way for me to not cease writing, however weary of collisions and seldom achieving détente. But perhaps this is what happened: despite the efforts and expectations of the readers, many writers ceased writing and are no longer present. And despite the efforts and expectations of the writers, many readers have given up their reading. I look into the tragic and phlegmatic face of poetry: why don't those voices continue? Did their writing just peter out? If reading is just a futile concomitant, then why do books like those still cry out to exist?

Naively reckless, I rise and fall with myself, up and down the hell of conversations that every ploughing up further confuses. Those expecting me to fail, those waiting for me to stand up, those wanting to see me survive. I respond by speaking, by silence, by falling down with a thud, by immense effort, by amusing myself, and by writing. There are stories that ask for a moment to heal, waiting for the presence of empathy. There are stories that attempt to speak. There are stories that have completely lost their naive enthusiasm and have received many persistent wounds.

I also bear in mind my own unavoidable shatterings, the polarized arguments that lead me to the realization that I can't achieve détente. Once again, I want to challenge myself, re-experiencing those wounds, those immature understandings, accepting and receiving those things that were and are to come, and gradually diminishing my fear, in order to give myself a chance to conclude, meaning an opportunity to begin again, an opportunity to depart and to move on.

I have not ceased doubting the necessity of the things I do, nor have I dared to believe that the pages I write have any worth. But no matter what, I have written something that I could not write now, something that I cannot rewrite, and, who knows, I may perhaps stumble upon the persistence not to give up reading and writing, here or there.

I may know what will not come back, but I don't know what will come. There are things that ought to be: I should be somewhere else in space, on a different axis, to understand the here and now. But there are also those concomitants of understanding: enduring, lingering, and opening the heart. To heal and be present. And finally, to take a step, deliberately, painfully, chafingly. And to abandon the desire to look back, because of the Orphean shadow there.

But if I don't look back, all those illusions in which I believed will also evanesce, and how will I know how fragmented I have become?

February, 2018
N.T.

[Un-]contextualizing Underground Poetry:
Reimagining a Critical Community

translated by David Payne

A Different Context

I first came to know another side of Vietnamese poetry, outside of the formal education system, through "virtual encounters," and friends in distant places: writers and works on internet forums like *Talawas, Tiền Vệ (Avant Garde), Evan (Electronic Literature), Da Màu (Colored Skin), Gió-O, Hợp Lưu (Confluence), Tạp Chí Thơ (Poetry Magazine)*, and overseas Vietnamese publications passed from hand to hand between friends inside the country. The circulation of these publications over many years even now tends to be associated with what is in Việt Nam (not just) humorously phrased "transmitting poisonous cultural products." At that time (2005), when I was timidly sending my own compositions to some online journals, the atmosphere of young poetry on those forums had reached its boiling point. Something extraordinary, unstable, even chaotic, as if a revolution was about to erupt. The storm was flowing out of Sài Gòn. Young poets and new poetry groups. Mở Miệng (Open Mouth). Ngựa Trời (Praying Mantis). Photocopy publishing. Resistance literature. Postmodernism. The writing of the generation of the '80s. After leaving University in 2007, and to a certain degree while writing for various State-run newspapers and magazines, I encountered yet another side of poetry: works and writers promoted in across familiar media channels that self-identified as "orthodox" or "the right side" and who somehow struggled to accept pluralistic ideas of literature. The stark contrast between these two sides can be captured, concisely and conclusively, and perhaps superficially, in the contrasting dualism: orthodox I unorthodox. Photocopy publishing, works printed overseas, and internet forums were ignored or one-sidedly criticized in the self-identified orthodox domestic media, all summed and labeled "unorthodox" solely for their means of publishing, and blocked in various ways by the cultural censorship authorities. However, it was these

21

"unorthodox" channels, oppressed and marginalized literature, those lacking acceptance, the small and strange voices, the underground presences that were both truly radical and experimental that appealed to me as manifestations of the effort to renovate art and the freedom of expression. The convection is there: hidden currents flowing under the surface, secret and concealed things, untamed, rebellious and disorderly, unorthodox (only) when compared to those things that were clearly revealed and were on display, presences that were controlled, curtailed, orderly, orthodox.

And yet I had the feeling that after these exhilarating crescendos of rebellion and debate in the early years of the new millennium, the atmosphere petered out within just a few years, silent and deserted, stagnant and exhausted, losing the rebellious creative context. I began to associate with literature at that awkward, inconclusive moment; the reck-lessness had dissipated, but a genuinely alternative context of Vietnamese literature had not yet become clear; there were only lone voices, short-lived stirrings, leaving me with a sad feeling that Vietnamese art and poetry had just let a real opportunity for change, a fierce determination to contribute its voice, slip through its fingers. I found myself dangling between two sides: not belonging anywhere, swinging back and forth between two yawning chasms, at risk of be sucked into an abyss.

That *artistic context*, once more, pushes me, a participant wanting to see themself in a multi-dimensional mirror, standing in front of a vast ocean, at the place where the waves are breaking, the waves of the past and the present crashing down. Would I now be able to sketch out more clearly the context of unorthodox literary and artistic voices in contemporary Việt Nam, and, more specifically, the context of underground voices in the poetry of the Post-Renovation period, those [self-] vanishing presences that are the topic of my interest here? Permit me to open a parenthesis: I tentatively use the designation Post-Renovation for the period from the 1990s until now, both to insinuate the alienation of so-called "Renovation" in Việt Nam and to chip away at the dominance of this term in the popular cultural discourse of the country. Frankly speaking, with only flimsy experience of life and literature, I do not aspire to persuade readers through an overview of the situation, supported by various statistics, descriptions, and sociological analyses of poetry. My overriding desire, within the limits of my own understanding, is to elicit attention and reflection on the context shared. The exploration of the context of [self-] vanishing presences in the poetry of this period, therefore, does not aim to stitch together the outer garments of social, cultural, and political events that clothe various movements, various phenomena, various authors, and their works, but rather to pay closer attention to the knots in the narratives, the weaving of poetry texts into larger socio-cultural texts, all of them interacting and colliding with each other, like the motion of electrons and the nucleus inside a molecule.

Without putting underground poetry into concrete conflict with mainstream poetry, I expect such things exist in parallel rather than opposition within the simplistic dualism of orthodox | unorthodox, and I would like to hypothesize that the wall that seems to divide these two separate worlds is only temporary. In its static sense, underground poetry is unorthodox, in *opposition* to the official orthodoxy connected to the control and backing of the state through the Vietnam Writers Association, the state publishers and the official media on literature and the arts. But in its dynamic sense, which I see as more significant, the diverse creative, publishing and interpretational activities of underground poetry are a counterbalance to orthodox poetry, as an endeavor of cultural criticism by artists on the margins; this criticism may lead to opposition and even heated confrontations with those things promoted by the state or it might reveal a seemingly aloof attitude in those pushing back against the commercialization of mainstream literature or both of these perspectives at the same time. I have more or less relied on terms such as *revolution* and *innovation*, or *revolutionary innovation*, even while questioning the extent of their applicability to this stream of underground poetry. Perhaps my concern is this: in Việt Nam, what is the context in which movements of ideological and aesthetic consciousness occur? And within this context, how do writers and artists position themselves and their works?

I want to emphasize that the analysis I provide below on the context of this movement is not intended to advocate for an explanation of underground poetry according to "special" local circumstances and it is even less an attempt to abet prejudices that more or less suppress the phenomenon of underground poetry—which seems in Việt Nam to be synonymous with "abnormal"—as simply being the inevitable consequence of "abnormal" and "special" socio-political circumstances. It would be too narrow-minded to view the existence of contemporary Vietnamese underground poetry as simply a kind of evidence of a dark side, representing the voice of helpless victims. It might also be too narrow-minded to understand the Vietnamese literary context only through attaching such wretched terms to the body of Vietnamese literature as post-war, post-colonial, or post-totalitarian. More than that, these analyses try to put underground art and poetry back into a relationship with orthodox art and poetry, a common pairing in every time and place that Việt Nam shares. Therefore, in my attempt at a discussion, the issues arising from this underground poetry should not be seen as an exotic flavor more or less designed to appeal to those far away, as a modish way of being modeled on discourses about a "prefabricated" context in non-Western countries, Third World countries or post-colonial countries | former colonies, but rather as a potential means of interrogating the participation of poetry and of poets in their local and historical context, a place where language can expose wounds to the air and require a progressively less fearful examination. And if I can take this further still, by locating underground poetry in its context, or by attempting to make visible these [self-]vanishing presences, I see this work of mine as both an effort to decontextualize poetry in order to reimagine a critical and renewed literary community, and as a way to share the story of (Vietnamese) literature today.

Post-Renovation: The Demand for a New Public Space

The attempt to identify the various factors that transformed the ideological and aesthetic template of the Post-Renovation period requires us to refer back to the Renovation period itself. Here, I pay attention to (i) the alienation of the term "Renovation," (ii) the decline of the role of orthodox fora and the creation of new spaces for new cohorts of writers, and (iii) the imagining of a possible community. I would like to acknowledge various analyses of basic conditions that lead to the affirmation of "the power of the powerless" as something far removed from the State system, the formation of un- or semi-official public spaces—stemming from the demand to expand civil society—and the emergence of critical independent intellectual qualities in Václav Havel's post-totalitarian society, interpretations that evoke valuable parallels with contemporary Việt Nam.[1]

Renovation and Post-Renovation

Excitement about literature during the Renovation period can be said to have begun with the 6th Party Congress in 1986, leading to a climax lasting around a year during 1988 and 1989. This brief period of time, as short as the "Beijing Spring," raised many issues that were discussed publicly in the state media, for example: creative freedom, the democratization of literature and art, and their independence from politics. Afterwards, this climax rapidly turned into an anticlimax due to the reimposition of a restrictive policy. The beginning of the decline can be said to be the Literature Congress of 1989, when the writer Nguyên

The Beijing Spring (Chinese: 北京之春; pinyin: Běijīng zhī chūn) refers to a brief period of political liberalization in the People's Republic of China (PRC) which occurred in 1978 and 1979. The name is derived from "Prague Spring," an analogous event which occurred in Czechoslovakia in 1968.

Nhã Thuyên

Ngọc, one of the Renovation pioneers, departed from the position of Chief Editor of the *Văn Nghệ (Arts and Letters)* newspaper. During the 7th Party Congress in 1991, General Secretary Đỗ Mười affirmed conservative thinking on literature and art, "repurposing" the definition of Renovation: "Our literature can only be Renovated in the correct direction, serving our people's Renovation cause according to the socialist orientation, under the leadership of the Party."[2] While the term "Renovation" remains popular in propagandist discourse and in discourse influenced by propaganda about the achievements of the "open door" cultural policy, a series of paradoxical events demonstrated its degeneration, revealing the difficult contradictions between the imperative of speaking the truth and living in the true situation of the country on the one hand that necessitates multiplicity, and the continued stifling grip of a single ideology on the other. Books were banned or prevented from publication. Their pages were carved up. The uncountable tragedies of the politicization of poetry. The lasting repercussions, and fates once thought to have been relegated to history. The banishments: those imprisoned just for circulating the poems of *Nhân Văn–Giai Phẩm*, like Hoàng Hưng, those who could not accept the Communist regime, like Nguyễn Chí Thiện, and the countless Southern poets who had been soldiers of the Republic and were incarcerated under the new regime, such as Tô Thùy Yên, Thanh Tâm Tuyền, and Trần Dạ Từ, so on and so forth. The overseas writers who were barred from entry, and the ever-growing list of

Nhân Văn–Giai Phẩm **affair:** a cultural-political movement for artistic freedom by writers, artists and intellectuals based in North Việt Nam which was launched in early 1955, later severely suppressed and officially ended in 1958. The movement revolved around two journals Nhân Văn (*Humanity*) **and** *và Giai Phẩm* (*Exquisite Works*). **Authors and those indirectly involved in this movement were disciplined, re-educated and banned from publishing for decades.**

26

Vietnamese writers and journalists receiving the annual Hell-
man/Hammett award, given to writers throughout the world
suffering political repression or human rights abuses.

This was also a period of international upheaval, including
the fall of the Berlin Wall in the autumn of 1989, the disinte-
gration of the Soviet Union and Eastern Europe, the reduction
of Soviet and Eastern European economic assistance to Việt
Nam in the late 1980s and early 1990s, the strong opposition
following the Tiananmen Square trauma in China, and Việt
Nam's normalization of relations with the United States in
1995, accession to the WTO, and the arrival of the internet,
all impacting art in Việt Nam in various ways. In the disap-
pointment over Renovation (that critics such as Lại Nguyên
Ân, Phạm Xuân Nguyên, and Đoàn Cầm Thi have shared in
various interviews and comments), in the alarm over the col-
lapse of the Soviet and Eastern European model, and the diver-
sification of foreign ideas, those working on art and literature
seemed to be standing in front of a half-open door ambiguously
labeled "Post-Renovation," none brave enough to find out what
was actually happening on the other side of the door. I would
like to recall an important article by the writer Phạm Thị Hoài,
a writer born during the war, who experienced life in North
Việt Nam as a young person, then emigrated to Germany, and
founded and edited the *Talawas* forum in which she looked back
on her own literary activities, reflecting on the relationship
between a writer and their era, describing the collapse of hope
in the Renovation, and naming this Post-Renovation period a
time "without a king" (borrowing the name of a short story by
Nguyễn Huy Thiệp):

> "The Post-Renovation period was a time of strange
> voids, absent authorities, carriages with neither
> locomotives or drivers. They kept on rolling, mostly
> sluggishly, until they ran out of momentum, through
> downhill stretches where they hurtled along at
> terrifying speeds, into steep ascents where they
> slowed and traveled backwards. The prestige of the
> old ideals, dogma and essential spiritual values had

been abandoned, but the void left behind had been sealed off, without giving way to a new prestige in its place. The guiding apparatus of the Party and of state control had lost its effectiveness, but a new operating system had not been permitted to accede to the throne. The top-down organizational structure was no longer effective, but a bottom-up union of individuals had not yet taken shape. Neither in previous decades nor in the Renovation period had Vietnamese writers taken individual initiatives and aspirations as a starting point to develop independent groups that could compete with the prestige of the organizations appointed and sponsored by the authorities."[3]

I admire Phạm Thị Hoài's profound and candid summary of the broken and disappointing relationship between the writers and the political institutions, which had its source in the literary and artistic life during the war as well as the ideological crisis that resulted from the prolonged subsidization of the creative sector in Việt Nam. This centuries-old arranged marriage, with the institutions taking the role of husband in a male-dominated society, had been shattered, but the yoke of both history and the present is so heavy that it is as if, in a collective unconsciousness, literature is still yoked to its status of either obsessively serving or resisting ideology, more or less continuing to maintain this strained relationship. But at the same time, I think that the "strange void" of the Post-Renovation period so sensitively perceived by Phạm Thị Hoài is not just a void of creative thinking, where the unified literature and art "under the leadership of the Party line," according to the unitary ideology of wartime that persisted into the Renovation period, faces crisis and collapse, but that void might also become a playground for destruction and regeneration, an arena for the flow of ideas and aesthetics, a place where the aspirations of groups or individuals can manifest and collide with each other. The final knell for the so-called Renovation has been sounded somewhere in Việt Nam, even though prominent individuals of this period still continue on their course in one way or another.

The mechanism of "subsidized ideology" has been broken down, and the power of the orthodox literary forums has been shaken. During the Renovation stage, writers and intellectuals, beginning with those deeply associated with the war such as Nguyễn Minh Châu and Nguyên Ngọc, once again, while demanding freedom for the arts, remained steadfast in their belief in institutions, a belief that was intensified when Secretary-General Nguyễn Văn Linh met with art and literature delegates at the beginning of the Renovation period in October 1987. The meeting is recognized in literary and artistic circles as symbolic of the excitement of the Renovation period. The declaration of the "loosening" of literature and art by the head of the Party leadership is seen as the launching of the movement of literary and artistic renovation, and a series of articles about these events appeared openly in the media.[4] But only a brief couple of years later, the direct relationship of the artists and progressive intellectuals with the authorities and the leaders of literature and the arts seemed to have weakened and their role had fewer opportunities to manifest itself. The *Văn Nghệ* periodical of 1987-1988, with the writer Nguyên Ngọc as Secretary-General, clearly reflected the transition from an official organ of the wartime government to an important forum for writers and intellectuals, with new debates and literary experiments, something both writers and readers had been expecting for many years; leading up to the present, especially for the majority of young people, this periodical has gradually become an anachronism, the image of an outdated ideology, resistant to change, and no longer worth worrying about. I think it would be fairer not to view these orthodox forums simply as propaganda agencies on literature and art. Perhaps, due to their commitment to ideological unity, they had to reconcile propagandistic aspects with the demand for truthful literature and art, a genuine demand that nearly always pushes any writer to a position that is distinct from or oppositional to the orthodox ideology of the state, particularly in those countries where the institutional model has not yet accepted pluralism of thought.

Nhã Thuyên

Internet Forums and New Spaces to Play

When the State's renovation pipedream is met with skepticism and the rules of the fora governed by privileged orthodoxy are no longer suited to creativity, the creative motivation will surely lead to a demand for alternative types of literary spaces — like a kind of self-awareness of Vietnamese literature about its own development. From here, I think it is necessary to look at the contribution of online forums and magazines as well as websites, personal blogs, and social networks in the formation of these alternative spaces for play. I would love to draw attention to the establishment and blossoming of overseas online literary magazines, run by exiled scholars and writers, in which a different outlook on a cross-border and global Vietnamese-language literature can be envisioned and grounded, regardless of the different directions and operating philosophies of each magazine, as typified by *Talawas, Tiền Vệ, Hợp Lưu, Tạp Chí Thơ, Gió-o,* and *Da Màu* that I mentioned above. Currently, such literary websites have mostly ceased to be active or are only sporadically updated, with only two literary magazines updated daily, namely *Tiền Vệ* and *Da Màu*. The ethos of Sydney-based *Tiền Vệ* is the question of the new, as they put on their website:

> The main aim of *TIEN VE* is to contribute to the formation of a Commonwealth of Vietnamese Arts, where, regardless of geographical and political differences, everyone can join and share their endeavor in exploration and experimentation so that artistic creativity is reunited with its original meaning, namely, the making of the new.

The ethos of US-based *Da Màu* is the question of colors: "Literature without borders: language, culture, gender, color, creed."[5] The Berlin-based *Talawas* (which implies the question *Ta là ai* | *who are we*) existed for a period of nine years (2001-2010) as a legendary forum in the field of Vietnamese literature, art, and progressive thought, and even though it has now ceased operations, the archived materials of this forum are still a valuable resource for research on Việt Nam in the past and the present.

I want to emphasize, in these forums, i.) the effort to digitize works that had been lost in war times and on the exiled journeys of writers, and the works erased from orthodox versions of literary history within the country compiled by specialists of state institutions, ii.) the support and encouragement of new literary trends, and iii.) in particular the effort to resurrect literary debate. The *Talawas* Bookshelf and the *Da Màu* Bookcase acted as open repositories for readers to freely consume books and materials that could not be officially disseminated within the country, particularly the records of "an inheritance of loss" (to borrow the title of a novel by Kiran Desai). A series of debates and questions revolved around topics prohibited in state communications, such as literature and politics, sexuality in literature, Southern literature, Nhân Văn–Giai Phẩm, war writings, feminism, human rights, cultural censorship about banned events, expurgated works, and so on. Self-publishing and the "Sài Gòn school of photocopied poetry" in the first years of the new millennium became a new brand of publishing, thanks to significant encouragement: the explosion of applause on *Talawas* for the self-publishing of Nguyễn Quốc Chánh, the introduction of a series of Sài Gòn photocopied poetry works and authors on Sunday *Talawas*, interviews of poets and readers on the topic of photocopied poetry on *Tiền Vệ* by the poet Trần Tiến Dũng in 2005, and many other articles. Introduc-

> Southern literature refers to the literatures published in South Việt Nam–officially the Republic of Việt Nam–which existed as a distinct country from 1955 to 1975 and comprised the southern half of what is now the Socialist Republic of Việt Nam. The Southern literature discussed here should not be conflated with what is considered "Văn học giải phóng miền Nam | The Liberated Southern Literature," mainly comprised of writers of the Communist party.

tions and translations of literary theories, of postmodernism, magical realism, feminism, post colonialism, and the likes from the West, rather than those from the Eastern Bloc, approached Vietnamese readers for the first time, raising more doubts on the singularity of literary theory coming from the State. Certain experiments appeared, for example visual poetry and multimedia poetry, on the webzines overseas.

Clearly, when the mainstream, in the forms of state media and commercial communication, doesn't support individual experimentation and is instead a vehicle for propaganda, these fora, despite constant firewalling and scrutiny, along with blogs, personal websites, and pervasive social networks, open up cyberspace and political emancipations, paving the way for diverse perceptions and practices. The attempt to create this unofficial public literary space, to recall the idea of Václav Havel in *The Power of the Powerless* discussed earlier, was also an attempt to create a literary civil society as a kind of theory and practice of "living in truth." Of course, there were misgivings, for instance regarding the transformation of literary spaces into political spaces, when outbursts of political protest in poetry seemed to drown out experiments and aesthetic debates. When literature is absorbed into polarized opposing ideologies and general human rights issues, then attention to its essential nature and to more private voices may be ignored or even suppressed. And this suppression, like all suppression, struggles to guarantee any such emancipation.

But it seems as if at some point, hopes were kindled about reconnecting Vietnamese writers scattered in all directions, and about a vision of contemporary Vietnamese literary life different from common conceptions of a literature long and heavily dependent on the state, closely tied to the "duty" of serving politics and propaganda: a democratization of literature taking shape, and endeavoring to be a part of world literature.

A Non-Generation Generation

This transformation that was I is going on slowly in overlapping waves is often described I denigrated using the terms "self-criticism" and "resistance." The effort to self-criticize and to "speak the truth" during the relaxing of regulations in the Renovation period, and the demand to "do normal art," eventually led to confrontations over freedom of expression. The phrase "self-criticism" ultimately came to sound like a form of compromise. The word "resistance," meaning to express dissident political views, became more prominent. According to the critic Phạm Xuân Nguyên, the word "resist" was originally a way for overseas Vietnamese authors to refer to writers inside the country who expressed attitudes that didn't conform to the official direction and line, breaking with the aesthetic of socialist realism of that time, for example found in the works of Dương Thu Hương, which those inside the country called "Nhân Văn 2 I Second Humanity"; afterwards, this word was often used to refer to the general literary phenomenon of divergent politics, not specific to those inside or outside the country.[6] But what followed after? Works banned for being "politically sensitive" perhaps only attracted a superficial tumult. Direct engagement with (the topic of) politics, to recall Jean-Paul Sartre's (perhaps now outdated or needing a revision) thesis on engaged literature, may become a reagent for self-respect and courage on the part of the poet, but it also carries the risk of turning literature into a local product sample, perhaps mass produced and of questionable quality. And what followed after? The unitary ideology that the State wanted to maintain through compulsory education has more or less become alienated, self-degraded, and mostly just empty propaganda as far as many young people were concerned. Commercial media encroaches on literary experimentation. Anxiety over political censorship and self-censorship parallel an equally great challenge: the power of censorship and seemingly invisible pressure by the market and the mass media. When Vietnamese writers are able to pursue a "normal" literary life, and it seems as if the limits of freedom extend infinitely, it may be that the bonds are harder to recognize, and therefore "censorship" is even not easily seen. The deliberate choice by writers and artists to marginalize themselves–though there might be some delicate distinction between the ones who are living for and with the margin and those who might want to approach the center in another way–formed a collective chorus of protest in the critical transition during the initial years of the Post-Renovation period, creating the need for a new effort on the part of the individual: to exist independently, often solitarily. But how to be an independent individual?

Older authors, identified with or influenced by the model of subsidized culture, were splintered by their choices in living and writing, either continuing in the role of "obedient children of the regime," or maintaining the illusion of renovation, searching for a way to "do literature" whilst in the pincers of the [a-]political discourse of the authorities regarding the arts, or falling into disillusionment, cynicism, and silence. A few became protesters, seeking an end to ambiguity in popular discourse, such as "you are free to write, as long as you don't impinge on politics," and were rapidly eliminated from official playgrounds. Younger writers growing up in a post-war and globalizing Việt Nam, especially in cities like Sài Gòn and Hà Nội, called for the renewal of literature and a "settling up" with the past. And perhaps there is now an even younger group still, those untroubled by the so-called past of literature or history, with the option of choosing a rootless, adventurous, meandering, and ambiguous mindset.

Is it possible to place hope in a generation of authors, typically described|denigrated a little too neatly in the term "new generation"? I want to insert a note of doubt here. The word "generation" always conveys the excitement of a shared change, companionship and coming together, in a tangled time of the old—the new, a time bursting with debates, manifestos, rebellions. But when those who used to rise and fall together in waves of literature and literary groups begin to splinter off, terms of classification and identity gradually become lifeless and exhausted, and we only see a few people toiling away in enclosed and isolated spaces, giving rise to the sensation of a poetic life that is undeniably cramped and stagnant, or a feeling of being adrift, outcast, and alone. For instance, should we file Nguyễn Quốc Chánh with the "post-war generation," or set him with the "generation of young Sài Gòn poets," or simply as a loner in the shadows? Is age important: do we have to speak of those born in the '70s or the '80s? We sense the disillusionment and self-criticism of a cohort of writers, the sense of loss and rootlessness of another cohort, and the deep disconnect and awareness of individual independence of the rising new class, but it is difficult to lump them together under the term "generation," in the illusion that a collective change is taking place. What it comes down to is that poetry does not have generations, or that this is a non-generation generation, just individuals, and these rootless individuals, adrift, seeking a place of refuge in some community, are perhaps always on the outside.

A Possible Community

The anxious concern and distant dreams about the possibility of this community are strongly related to whether writers and readers can gradually erase separation and ambiguity, clearing away the detritus obscuring the portrait of Vietnamese contemporary poetry, by both listening to the voices of living poets and tending to dead souls.

This community will be even less possible if the malignant tumors of the past are not fully acknowledged, two large tumors seem to have been erased from orthodox accounts of literature and the arts: the Nhân Văn–Giai Phẩm movement in the North and the legacy of the Southern literature under the former Republic. The official re-printing of some poetic materials that were considered to be underground in the past, and the concurrent official recognition of poets who suffered due to the Nhân Văn–Giai Phẩm affair, such as Lê Đạt, Trần Dần, Phùng Quán, and Hoàng Cầm through State prizes for literature and arts (in 2007, when Trần Dần had already passed away), have more or less made them more known to readers today, although for poets the choice of whether or not to accept recognition by the state and the legitimacy of these awards is also controversial. But this state loosening is still not sufficient. Many writers of "the past South" and all the "dark" and "gloomy" compositions of wartime literature continue to be cast aside. Traditions have been broken, and literary wounds have never been reopened and healed, thoroughly and unambiguously, so that writers and readers can step forward in literature with a clearer past. The past, in a certain sense, engages deeply with the contemporary in its essential traumas, and therefore a need to look back and reformulate a more justifiable and balanced history of (Vietnamese) literature erratically emerges.

This community will be even less possible if there are still geographical divides in the way that contemporary Vietnamese literature is viewed, more precisely the Hà Nội-Sài Gòn divide (not Hồ Chí Minh City as indicated on the maps, a name that seeks to erase history and the past by using the name of the winner of one phase of history) and the domestic-overseas divide. There is a mythical Sài Gòn, and an attempt to revive that myth amongst writers and readers here: not just as the former Pearl of the Orient, the most modern city in Southeast Asia, but also the myth of freedom in publishing and in literature and the arts, with the flowering of movements and groups before "reunification" with the North. Sài Gòn has become a symbol of alternative culture in the first years of the 21st century, a space of marginalized and unorthodox poets, of opposition and refusal, and of efforts for innovation and creativity. Hà Nội, the land of "a thousand years of civilization," possesses another myth, a label I consider not completely justified, equating it with the space of power, a conservative and stagnant place where orthodox poets keep a tight grip on literary circles, with little room for exploration. The divide between Hà Nội as the center and Sài Gòn as the margins, like the domestic-overseas divide, seems up until now to only signify a prolonging and deepening of the sequelae of a harsh separation, a massive historical trauma that is not yet fully understood. This divided past still pervades the present: the migration of Hanoians to Sài Gòn in 1954, the evacuation of

Vietnamese in Sài Gòn to California, and sites in Australia and other countries, the long period with the two regions under two regimes (1954-1975), and the fratricidal wars, "the winner" and "the loser." Can literature and poetry participate in the effort to heal and eradicate those walls?

This community would be even less possible if those divided pairs become fixed terms, frozen statues. Until now, many people still default to the idea that contemporary underground poetry in Việt Nam only includes or is equivalent to the term Sài Gòn Young Poetry, like the brand of a rebellious early 21st movement. This perspective exposes a geocentric view of culture, which only pays attention to the geographical location of alternative movements. In reality, these geographic boundaries have been broken, blurred by authors, texts, and readers coming together in cyberspace and in underground-independent publishing networks rather than in locations where they may temporarily reside. So-called Vietnamese contemporary poetry has expanded its scope, not just inside Việt Nam, but also across borders, associated with Vietnamese communities that are keeping Vietnamese writing alive in many places throughout the world. One more unjust and misunderstood aspect on the part of the reading community is the identification of underground poetry and its simple reduction to "dissident poetry": poets bearing the brand of dissident, those raising their voice to demand freedom and democracy for the country and its people rather than the themes of literary exploration, and literature as a means of aggressive friction rather than open flow of insight.

By overcoming these divisions and preconceptions, acknowledging the oppression and the oppressed, contemporary Vietnamese poetry might open up richer and more abundant spaces, with a clearer sense of hope for a more critical and sharing community. There, regardless of idealized expectations, writers and readers would be able to do away with the artificial division between literature and politics, to eradicate the subordination of writers to the authorities, and to come together in a "normal" literary community as a place of creativity and interpretation that is passionate for the criticism of rigid norms and corrupted aesthetics.

Yet Another Context

The collision between poetry, poets, and their context, and the attempt to envision a community, prompt me [plural] to interrogate the potential participation of poetry. I don't know whether it is possible, in societies where the demand for political action by the masses seems more urgent than the demand for literary creation, to contemplate a successful connection between literature (distinct from propaganda) and politics? Is resistance itself a form of innovation in or against a certain context, and vice versa? Can individual and collective practices both mirror each other and participate in the same process of becoming? I still persist in considering how the political dimensions of language are different from calls to march in the streets, and that writers have to work to justify their existence apart from their own experience and practice, their own words. It's on the page, poetry can locate its relationship with its time in its own distinct experience of language, and the interrogation of the condition of language may, in turn, shape the poet.

> Editorial Note: The page both epitomizes and resolves into multiplicities the tension between the individual (as both autonomous being and fantasy amidst the throes of circumstance and power) and the collective (itself a fantastical mass and an already-present dynamic force).

I had wanted to observe more closely the trap in which writers in Việt Nam are stuck. The pressure they are facing seems to originate not only from their preoccupations as writers, but also from the eagerness of the readers, the citizenry, for writers to cease taking pleasure in "pure" aesthetics and playing with words, and to participate in "changing life" (to quote Arthur Rimbaud). I don't know if this can be seen as a consequence, but over the past decade or so, many prominent poetic identities seem to have chosen to disappear, to fall silent, leaving behind only unsettling questions and a feeling of loss on the part of the readers, when they seem to see writing poetry and pursuing a life in poetry as futile pursuits, and when they themselves are spinning in circles, or being spun around, by questions of responsibility and participation. I think more about the right of poets to be silent and to disappear. The poets will say: I write for readers in the here and now, not for some illusory future. The poets will also say: even if I don't (write in order to) shut my eyes and cover my ears, to escape or to sketch illusory hopes, I still want to believe that poetry has no social responsibility other than to seek its own path to self-emancipation. Does literary writing, and those who write it, have to be attached to something, or can they choose not to adhere to a narrow framework, to remain homeless and even to play with the nihilism of having no refuge at all, when being anchored hinders creativity? I imagine the moment when the/a/ each poet looking for themself/herself in a strange mirror, they/she see only a face twisted and erased, multiple images cancelling each other out, buffeted by the waves of endless events and voices, and they/she a singular body, strives to retrace their/her steps in order to identify the point at which they/she become a part of the mirrored-world, and how to preserve their true faces.

I believe that the pulse of literature and of poetry is always vitally linked to the time and space in which it exists, but poets may beat to a deeper pulse still: in their soul, in their reading, in their encounters, in journeying and wandering through cultures, in their dreams of reviving long-forgotten pasts, in discovering hitherto unseen visions of the present in a ray of fragile hope, and in attending to the possibilities of language. My concern about the interrogations of language arising from these poetic practices, therefore, prompts my caution regarding the mythologized earth-shattering potential of dissenting poetry in Việt Nam, frequently reduced to mere political protest poetry, (supposedly) attracting overseas attention and being increasingly exploited, while aesthetic interrogations may be diminished or set aside. I want to persist in clinging to this cherished aspiration when I endeavor to observe, and to a certain extent understand, the [self-]vanishing presences in contemporary Vietnamese-language poetry, with the humble expectation that the face of this poetry will gradually be unmasked (the poetry will gradually be unveiled): poetry cannot just be the continuing testimony of those suffering from ideological conflicts during unfortunate periods in the history of a people. There would be no hope to have an equal conversation if Vietnamese literature doesn't bring new voices and unique poetic identities if it only knows how to come like a far-off flavor of political variables. I imagine that the process of peeling back that mask has been and is going on, in the shadows, with no little pain, its direction unclear, with the detritus of the past and the present, of ideologies and literary attitudes, and perhaps there isn't any other way.

I don't know if it is overly ambitious to raise the possibility of creating a different image of post-war Việt Nam, a different image of a dissident Việt Nam in the Renovation and Post-Renovation period, a more expansive image of Việt Nam with the diverse literary trends of the present and an as yet unknown projection. In poetry, the process of dismantling a monopolistic ideology and participating in it occur simultaneously, and the existence of underground poetry, of [self-]vanishing presences, is not in fact in opposition to orthodox poetry, "state poetry," and "state literature," but aims to stimulate poets and poetry in general. The condition of being marginalized, whether as a deliberate choice or not, can nourish an emancipated grammar of poetry, and can actually empower those who submerge themselves in the life of language. These are voices, endlessly seeking to share and sincerely cherishing the hope of a community of their own.

Womxn's Poetry: A Resonance of Voices
translated by Kaitlin Rees

The Mirror Illuminating Me

What my body says: no, I do not want acts of reading and writing to be totally enclosed inside frames of gender, I do not want poetry to be attached to the words "male" or "female," "homo" or "hetero"—such labels burden me with the same heaviness of facing the excessive amounts of luggage I carelessly packed for a long journey. Yet I also hear a different whispering: stories that seem to originate *from* and flow *into* only the experiences of womxn authors. When knocking at the doors of small private homes kept by womxn poets, when pressing an ear to their secluded walls, at times I feel the joy of free solitude, at times it is a solitude so resolute it becomes impossible to penetrate. At times when knocking, it is only the echo of my own vague knocking that I hear, at times when pressing my ear to their walls, it is only the breath of deserted moss that I feel. Other times I hear a scream, a strange shrieking, a shattering, a wall cracking, a rock dropped, a sob, a wail, a whimper, an arrogant laugh, a hopeless scattering of oneself down into the depths of an imaginary chasm. And whenever my ear is struck by an explanation, an analysis, an

EN: What surrounds the private? When imposed, forced into, it removes one from the public, from interstitial life, partitioned off from the whole. Yet private becomes also public spectacle—to be seen under disciplined conditions, but not to see. But what of a chosen private, an impossible glimmer of utopia, to exist outside of disciplining conditions, of imposition? Where "lone presence" is able to give way to collective awakening. We see free and forced solitude aggress each other, both as felt realities and impossible fantasies, divorced from and always in dialogue with the public.

emphatic declaration or condemnation, I can still feel how sensation and imagination prickle the skin of womxn bodies. My body naturally trembles, in a shared breath or in distance admiration. For such reasons, I choose to use the provisional label of "womxn's poetry" within the space of this essay, and I choose to observe the [self-]reflected images of womxn poets in closest proximity to the *feminine*: narratives of the body. A wavering posture: the deepest privacy of a body itself, a body refusing to shoulder all messages, a body "nỗi riêng lớp lớp sóng dồi," " innermost feelings surge in layers layers of waves," "một mình mình biết một mình mình hay," in which "one self one knows well one self's self," to borrow some expressions from the poetry of Kiều, here becomes a way of expressing, becomes one who exposes, becomes a storyteller, and, often, becomes a vehicle of messages that intend to be visible.

In Vietnamese, the word for "women" is composed of two parts: "phụ" and "nữ," from the Chinese "婦"and "女," in which "phụ" refers to womxn with husbands, and "nữ" refers to womxn without husbands, thus locating womxn inside their familial relations. Here and throughout this essay, I use "nữ" by itself (without the "phụ") as an intentional navigating outside the constraints of familial relationships and thereby placing men and womxn, the masculine and the feminine, in positions of (assumed) equality regardless of differences in sexuality and body.

The authors I touch upon here—though perhaps not the (womxn) poets most in accordance with my personal

Translator's Note: Paralleling Nhã Thuyên's wish to reimagine a word as a means to reimagine its socially binding relationships and oppressive context, I wish to write "woman" or "female" without the presence of "man" or "male" as its component part. Considering "womyn", "femme", "lady", I decide on "womxn" for its step away from the biblical concept of women as being a subset of men, and for its inclusivity of trans-womxn and womxn-identified groups.

taste–share a common story in which I am more or less impli-
cated. I envision their choice to write as a way of exhibiting a
feminine experience
and–with sharp and
direct intentionality–
engaging in the process
of rejecting womxn as
reflected objects and,
instead, asserting their
self-reflected subjec-
tivities. In dialogue
with the insurgencies
of past writers, their
works have grown up
with a strong aware-
ness of protest against
oppressive societal
structures, toiling to
reimagine womxnhood
in order to create a
visible presence of fem-
ininity and elicit hope
for a community of Vietnamese womxn writers. At the very
least, that is one story in recent Vietnamese literature that can
be opened.

> EN: Integral to Nhã Thuyên's
> work, it is crucial to disrupt
> oppositional, binarist think-
> ing. Here, femininity does not
> stand in stark opposition to
> masculinity but rather encom-
> passes and explodes the
> binary. Femininity can con-
> tain masculinity and gender
> non-comformity, and it holds
> open space for future work
> towards this capacious poeth-
> ical sensibility, gaps within
> which one can glimpse queer
> and trans privacies and pub-
> lics, other complex textual life
> that contents with patriarchal
> normativities.

    Around the turn of the century, it seemed as if some
Vietnamese readers were expecting a wave of womxn's poetry
with authors carrying radical concepts within their written
art, a confluence of those inside and outside the country, of
several ages in succession. Notably, those living abroad: Lê
Thị Thấm Vân, Lê Thị Huệ, Nguyễn Thị Thanh Bình, Nguyễn
Thị Hoàng Bắc, Nguyễn Thị Ngọc Nhung, Trịnh Thanh
Thủy, Đỗ Lê Anhdao, Miên Đáng and Trần Minh Quân.
As with those living in Việt Nam: Dư Thị Hoàn, Ý Nhi, and
the younger poets Ly Hoàng Ly, Phan Huyền Thư, Nguyễn
Thúy Hằng, with the Ngựa Trời group–Thanh Xuân, Lynh
Bacardi, Khương Hà, Phương Lan, and Nguyệt Phạm. Within
these sets, some illustrate the blunt demand for womxn's rights,

while other voices are seemingly apolitical, exploring the experiences of the imagination, and refusing to express any clear message. The voice of the body, of the imagination, notions of love, sexuality, self-definition—how can such private concepts grow into a shared story of womxn's poetry? How can the lone presence of an individual beside another, and another, come to awaken a consciousness of suppression, and in turn, demand the resistance to such suppression? When do power relationships need critical reflection, between female and male, womxn and men, womxn writers and men writers, womxn writers and their societal structure, womxn writers and themselves, or, more essentially, the enduring inequality between the presence of femininity and masculinity? Though I have not yet had the fortune of surveying many original voices from the pens of womxn writing in Vietnamese, I believe there have been notable interrogations of the prejudices placed on womxn and their representation in Vietnamese literature in the past as well as the currently passing period, giving presence to a distinct feminine experience and essence, enabling the feminine disposition to transform into a thriving vitality of language.

I Am a Lady: Grass in a Game of Wind

The image of womxn protesting masculine discourses rooted in the heavy yokes of patriarchal rule emerges across numerous pages of womxn's writing in candid language and poetic message. There are only four womxn authors who appear in the unique collection *26 Contemporary Vietnamese Poets*, published by Tân Thư Publishing House in the USA in 2001, including (outside Việt Nam) Nguyễn Thị Hoàng Bắc, Lê Thị Huệ, (inside Việt Nam) Ly Hoàng Ly, and Phan Huyền Thư; nonetheless, the theme of agitating for feminism—particularly within the poetry of Nguyễn Thị Hoàng Bắc and Lê Thị Huệ— leaves a provocative impression. I take pleasure in Nguyễn Thị Hoàng Bắc for her distinctive tone: bemused humor in great sorrow, levity in deep compassion, quietly mocking, ready for attack, yet seeming to maintain something poetic.

Betrothal

slap bang
the drum beat of betrothal   rumbles
its drum roll call to battle
her escorting hour is up   and then what
to the ends of the earth
what will I do   with that man guy there
     and

what will it do to me

the drum beat of betrothal
banging the beat of battle
hackneyed speech the minister speaks
from this day on til forever
two lives shall be   fused
everlasting conjugal irons
shoulder to shoulder, back braced
standing
together on the frontlines

me and that puppet man there
the drum beat pries the arms open
a pair of eyes regards the other
bloodshot and strained

Here, the image of a solemn and sacred bridal reception, in accordance with traditional customs, a symbolic image of hierarchy and ritual in which conceptions of love and marriage converge, gets desanctified through permutations of vocabulary: the words describing the marriage betrothal ceremony simultaneously represent an actual battle—where the betrothal drum becomes the battle drum, the scene of exchanging vows is represented as "bloodshot and strained"—and the scene of enduring togetherness as "together on the frontline." A transformation of the womxn's condition from passive to active arises out of a change in perspective of the object: reaching the end

45

of the poem, "that man guy there" is merely "that puppet man there," the object with an ability to dominate (man) is turned into a passive figure, a phantom (puppet). With a seemingly lighthearted poem, Nguyễn Thị Hoàng Bắc has, on one hand, subverted the hierarchical relations between husband and wife as a first step to their reaching an eye-to-eye equality, and on the other, unmasked through parody a system of language that oppresses womxn from its unconscious use. The battle may be dramatic—"bloodshot and strained"—but it is not loud, and for that the poem is, in a differently illuminated meaning, truly romantic.

In another poem, Nguyễn Thị Hoàng Bắc reverses the condition of womxn being pinned into the figure of "she whose piss cannot surpass the tips of grass" with a bold reinterpretation of this act. The poem "Tips of Grass," first appearing in *Hợp Lưu* magazine in 1997 and later reprinted in the aforementioned anthology, erupted in a scandal of womxn "pissing poetry":

Tips of Grass

the sound of piss
                    dripping drips
trickles in a toilet
warm liquid quivers
                                  amber
streams from body
yeah
I'm a lady
the category of she whose piss cannot surpass the tips of grass
now
able to bask on this grand throne
later it'll be us
who fatten our pot bellies thick
this trickling like rain
this wind's game trembling the grass tips

This poem stirs me; scornfully proud and truly intimate, mocking and sympathetic, even tender, it is both a challenge to and a confession of one's plight. The image of a "lady" listening to the sound of her own trickling piss, the quivering amber liquid streaming out of her body, her self-described "grand" posture on the toilet, and the re-performance of her bodily gestures without the slightest bit of shame, such images come together to produce an effect of an irreverent playfulness, a humorous and intelligent negation of the feminine principles that tend to govern by way of the masculine gaze and womxn's allegiance to it. The pleasure of playing with one's own excrement (piss), the self-observation, and its exhibition of and in a private space (the bathroom) create a complex of images and acts that reveal a naturally wild and freely-expressed joy. It is quite different from the works

EN: What would it be like to view oneself in relation only to oneself? What vision of self emerges when one experiments in language with removal from violent power relations? How might a womxn understand herself outside of men, outside of her relation to and entanglement with patriarchy? Of course, this is a task futile as it is necessary, through which other visions of possible life and possible collective thought and life.

in contemporary art that use similarly "dirty" materials in order to manifest ambitious and more shocking ideas; one is reminded of *Merda d'Artist/Artist's Shit* of Pierre Manzoni or *Shit Show* of Andres Serrano, for example. The grotesquely imagined and exaggerated image of a womxn who "fattens [her] pot belly thick" as a result of "bask[ing]" on the toilet, a womxn who produces a "trickling like rain" liquid stream, perhaps can be read as an allegory of disobedience, but it is one with a light-heartedness that opens itself up to wonderment. It would be less possible to comprehend all the nuances of humor in this poem without reimagining the more traditional spaces of village life for Vietnamese womxn in the past, where the modern bathroom had yet to appear and toilets might simply be a deserted space in the middle of a field—privacy performed in the middle of a public space, as opposed to a toilet's private space in modern life. In this vein, the poem creates a contentious liminal space between private and public, traditional and modern, rural and urban, with the act of a woman's self-gaze clearly not detached from a sense of reinterpreting the past and the space of the past. If this process of unmasking is understood as a form of antagonism, then it is a challenge with many targets: not only are the masculine gaze and societal structures called on for reinterpretation, but the living spaces themselves, as well as the oppressions that are tacitly embedded in language. The act of making poetry, self-revealing one's condition through language, is not a treatment for one individual psyche to satisfy its need for expression; it is an energizing against the current in search of some origin. The effort to demolish the prison walls surrounding an individual becomes no less important than that of demolishing the prison walls surrounding a wider community.

Red Flag of the Pelvis & Exiled Bodies

Before going on to discuss a different theme of womxn's poetry, allow me to recall one point that sparked a feminist debate within the Vietnamese writing community in 2005 regarding an incident of appropriation of the (womxn's) body in writing. The heart of the storm could be found in a series of games inspired by the editors of *Tạp Chí Thơ* in the Spring Issue 2005 themed "(I am) the Center of the Universe." The editors concocted exercises that asked the navels of 26 poets (of any gender) to tell their poet's story in freely written poems about the body, in conjunction with a "Guess Who" quiz on the publication's website (now deactivated), which operated as a game for readers to guess which poets have "happily flaunted their navels to the world" by clicking on those navels. Other games included the use of body images, such as "Body Stall", "Pelvic Gates" and "Red Flag of the Pelvis," each creating an animated party on the body and to provoke certain contrary reactions.

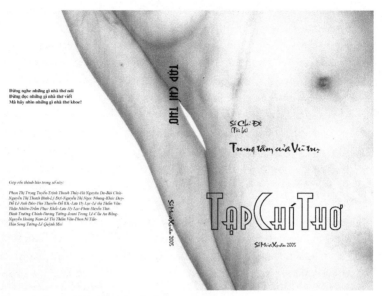

Image 1: Cover of Tạp Chí Thơ, Spring Issue 2005.

The most extreme reaction was that from a feminist group of womxn writers named Nguyễn Trần Khuyên, a combination of Nguyễn Vũ Khuyên and Trần Minh Quân, with an essay entitled "A Literature Constructed by the Masculine and Serving the Masculine." It presented two clear arguments: a criticism of the "phallocentric" works of men authors appearing in the online forums of *Tiền Vệ* and *Talawas*, and criticism of the womxn authors who participated in *Tạp Chí Thơ*'s games, asserting that their work was representation of "a literature serving masculinity—the lack of a feminist consciousness and culture in womxn's writing." Regarding "phallocentricism," the group provided a critical statistic from their research: "images that invoke sex and the female body for the purpose of expressing political and social views comprise around 70% of writing...Thus, one risk in the struggle for freedom and innovation is the direct insult of womxn by men authors who treat them as mere sex things, no more and no less."[7] (Nguyễn Trần Khuyên). As for feminine acquiescence, the group contested that the act of womxn authors putting their navels on display

Nhã Thuyên

was the manifestation of superficial feminist consciousness both trapped inside and reinforcing the "tradition of phallicism." Subsequently, Nguyễn Trần Khuyên then initiated a petition to collect signatures for an *Against Misogynist Literature Campaign*, demanding that *Tạp Chí Thơ* remove from their website the abusive images that "expose womxn's bodies as packaged goods to satisfy the sexual instincts of men." Putting aside these sharply conflicting ideas around men and womxn writers, I found that this essay raised insightful points that could be further debated. It was a distinctly feminist voice in conversation with previously initiated debates such as the womxn authors of *Tạp Chí Thơ* in the late 1990s, *Tạp Chí Việt (Việt Magazine's)* early 2000 issue themed "Love, Sexuality and Gender," *Tiền Vệ*'s issue themed "Love and Sexuality in Literature," as well as opening up future debates including the criticisms put forth by the Ngựa Trời group, themes of sexuality appearing in *Da Màu* and so on. Evidently, there was a marked impact of sexual encounters on the overall literary landscape of this period.

I consider the compatibility of an idea put forth in "Rethinking the Public Sphere: A Contribution to the Critique of Actually Existing Democracy" by Nancy Fraser. By identifying Jürgen Habermas's idealized nature of the bourgeois public sphere and the blind spot of gender and masculinity in conceiving of that public sphere, Fraser recognizes the coexistence of competing public spheres of marginalized communities who are often excluded, as exemplified in the womxn she categorizes as "counterpublics." The somewhat impromptu feminist groups mentioned above could be seen as efforts to resist exclusion from literary public spaces in and outside Việt Nam. I wonder, if in the pressurized politics of Việt Nam's human rights context in general, a wider dispersal of individual voices on gender or race issues result in those voices becoming weaker, possibly misinterpreted, or pushed impossibly far aside?

Returning to the works of womxn poets, it is possible to see the outbreak of narratives about|from the human body, with themes of sexuality shaping the rediscovery of an exhibited self, as a means of effectively awakening to—and thus confronting—the suppressing power of social bias. To a certain extent, the [self-]liberated body voice—emerging in both gleeful rediscoveries and in manifestations of pain—could be read as a textual strategy to attack popular Eastern patterns of beauty and femininity that often value the silent suffering and the hidden. Making more or less grotesque aesthetic choices can disrupt the habitual use of decorative images of feminine beings and, necessarily, disrupt the enjoyment | consumption of feminine beauty according to the preferences of the "customer." How does it feel for womxn to expose a part of their body perceived as taboo? Is it a joy to discover and possess one's own skin? Does it feel shameful? Is there a cold indifference? Or the rising bravery of a warrior? Lê Thị Thấm Vân delightfully displays the little hairs of her armpit in a photo of her body:

EN: These affects contort, fold in on themselves, overflow. Shame gains a possible glint of a triumphant joy, where exhibiting that which ought be hidden and private becomes not merely a subversion of private-public but a subversion of affective ordering as well, delightful display.

Raise Your Hands If
thank you to the poet Đỗ Kh.

I have (had to) raise my hand
to ask please
to say here
to agree
to surrender
to express a view

Nhã Thuyên

among so many other
to's.
Now I (am) lying down
raising my hand to
proclaim the little hairs
have newly sprouted from my armpit,
and that's it.

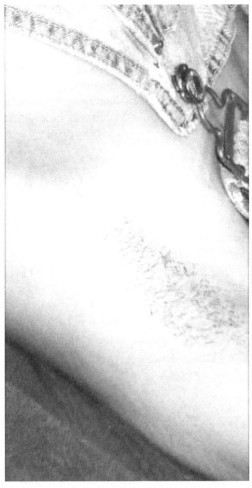

Image 2: Image in the poem.

Five female poets of the Ngựa Trời group appear on the cover of the poetry anthology, *Dự báo phi thời tiết (Forecast of Non-weather)*, in an intentionally shocking image that gave reason to the Vietnamese cultural censorship office to issue a ban on the book's circulation shortly after its release.

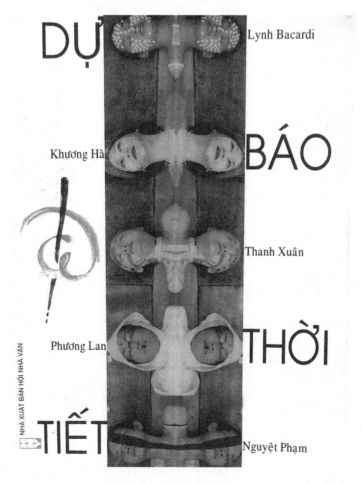

Image 3: Cover of poetry collection Dự báo phi thời tiết (Forecast o Non-Weather) (Writer's Association Publishing House, 2006)

And a narrative that seems the utmost personal and slight, "Two Moonly Ones in the Nude" by Trần Minh Quân—one of the initiators of the aforementioned feminist group Nguyễn Trần Khuyên—carries a touching revelation of the body. A few drops of blood, the sound of dripping water, two naked bodies, languid yet teeming with energy of the imagination:

Two Moonly Ones in the Nude

Pre-arrival of the blood clots my mind
two of us lie naked and listen to the tub's drip
to answer the question of a damp morning:
Yes, her body is motion.
It clung to the chance when I slipped
holding my hand longer than politeness
with the message of a craving to kiss my clothes (for covering my
body).
From behind she's breathing question marks into my ear,
though the only thing I can comprehend
is the distance between my hand and her lips.
Yes, her entire body, a dislocated craving,
eyes nose, hand leg, cigarettes she smokes –
flying high then clinging to me.

On a different side of inspiration, unoccupied with bodily hedonism, Lynh Bacardi leaves a deep impression of cruelty's hysteria, a sorrowful ache for the grim existence of a body, particularly inside psychological disorder:

By Birth

her grace is thirty years old
a birthmark at the edge of her left eye
I detect the scent of blood on her body
the night sky reeks of sewer pipe
needles bend beneath the soles of her feet
her grace so slowly descends the stairs
a visionless gaze

a street ablaze and the shriek of sirens
her mother appears murdered in the bedroom
hands still holding a mechanical dick

blood drips from the stairs

her grace is thirty years old

The body's dark secret and the exposure of libido follow
Lynh Bacardi's harsh language as means of violent protest
against oppressive institutions. Impressions of blood on the
body, its smell, traces of blood on the stairs, the death of her
mother with a sex toy in hand, the needles beneath the soles
of her feet—all are signs of the body's stimulation, dense with
urban material, a horrifying and heartless state of inhumanity,
an animalistic chaos in daily living space, where those who
bear the brunt of suffering, are womxn. In this place and else-
where, I hear echoes of Eve Ensler's *The Vagina Monologues*. A
minor note: the "*The Vagina Monologues*" by Eve Ensler has been
translated in its entirety by Hoàng Ngọc-Tuấn, with several
excerpts published during the time of *Tiền Vệ* magazine's theme
of "Love and Sexuality in Literature."

To explore instinct, to fuel the needs of the body, writing
about love and sexuality become themes with a humanitarian
perspective—something belonging to people (womxn in par-
ticular) who suffer a repressed longing, those groping in the
dark to recover the secrets of their vitality. The passionate
and instinctual selves of Lê Thị Thấm Vân or Phương Lan
exemplify this concentrated strength of sexual impressions and
emotional intensity. And still, there is a political story that adds
something darker. There is "Freedom's Cost" by Lê Thị Thấm
Vân, a work about sexuality that does not suggest a passionate
attachment or crazy romance, but rather, evinces something
vulgar, violent, stressful, a perspective of the oppressed that
challenges by exposing tragedies:

Nhã Thuyên

Freedom's Cost

The night before I fled by sea
mother lit incense and mumbled a prayer
god help my child get away
from police
from imprisonment
from the hungry fish
from the beasts of bronzed faces, square chins, scowling eyes,
smacking
 their lips out on the open sea.

But god goes blind eyed, plugged eared, about-face.
A girl of tender age
three times suffers
nine dicks spitting slimy seed on vagina-eyes-lips-mouth-
hair-ear-belly-thigh-breast…

The body of a teenage girl
is a delicious feast for the fish
under the tender evening light.

Explicit and clear in its message, the poem is a testimony of
the fate of exiled bodies. I don't know the past realities experi-
enced by these refugee womxn writers; however, their writing
calls back the scars of hard-won freedom and its expensive
cost, recognizing the trampling of one's body. The demand for
human rights (freedom) that obstructs womxn's rights (sadistic
suffering) destabilizes the poem between suppressive forces.
The final image, the body of a teenage girl becoming a feast
for fish under the soft light of a full moon, induces the violent
grief that encompasses abuse. The literal representation of a
womxn's painful experience of crossing the sea in this poem,
or the use of a militaristic lexicon as a device to parody war-
time language in the previously discussed poems by Nguyễn
Thị Hoàng Bắc, allows the reader to open the subject of
feminism up to another subject: a nation's story. The condition of
womxn-as-sufferer here can be placed in a genealogy of

mythologized images that have transformed Vietnamese womxn into a people, a nationality, in which they are not only the victims of traditional ideas and social structures as dictated by a patriarchy, but also continue to the be victims who are appropriated to serve a nationalist discourse. Recalling here the film *Surname Viet, Given Name Nam* by Trinh T. Minh-ha (1989, USA), the echoes of these drifting bodies resonate in history.

Feminine Existence: A Resonance of Voices

Arriving here, I want to shift back to a more distant past, to dig into a deeper layer of soil in order to understand the genealogy of Vietnamese womxn poets and poetry written about womxn, not excluding those representations shaped | sanctioned by a male gaze. But perhaps to be more practical, and potent, I will just highlight one story that is gradually slipping into the recent past, to see the stages of birthing labor as no less painful for the Vietnamese womxn authors who self-reproduce new poetic beings. This is also a place where the story of equality can be re-interrogated and broadened. *Feminism | womxn's rights | femininity* are words that do not (just) continue to battle for gender equality—a battle that perhaps ends in a stalemate as it repeats and replicates, if enacted with the central idea of violence, the popular hyper-masculine model that tends to assert powerful ambitions to establish order and control—no, these words also reside in their endeavor to confront the control and mastery performed by those male characteristics (without confronting men). At the same time, feminism resides in the rewrite and affirmation of feminine existences, making femininity visible and engaged in a dialogue that initiates journeys to [self-]emancipation from violent repressions. Equality lies not in the identifying words that denote worn-out threads—recalling that a certain weariness accompanies matters of "male" or "female", men or womxn, men writers or womxn writers, womxn's rights or men's rights; rather, equality lies in the ability to escape the grips of violent power relationships.

Nhã Thuyên

In poetry after the American War in Việt Nam, readers heard a crescendo rising to a boom that called for a *womxn's voice* to speak out in the poetry of womxn authors. This can be considered the first wave of an awakening feminine presence here, yet it is easy to concur that this was a feminine self-positioning within I attached to I snugly fit inside the framework of masculinity. As a result of being pushed into the blind spot of gender, of being masculinized or asexualized during a period of prolonged war, the post-war poetry of womxn authors like Lâm Thị Mỹ Dạ and Lê Thị Mây—writers who had linked themselves to revolutionary movements—were later full of private anxieties about the post-war fate of womxn: the need to be a mother, to be a normal wife, the need to be loved and reaffirm love with acceptance or even praise of the "female duties" which typically referred to a simple collection of indicators pointing to one's personal life in the cramped spaces of family and cooking. They patiently console themselves while waiting for soldiers in battle: "The woman I am came back to sewing / skillfully embroidering and stitching clothes for kids." They endure the swallowing back of tears: "Night after night of embroidered silence / Not only me who bears this, a he who does not return" (Lê Thị Mây, "Titleless"). At times we can hear alternate voices, screams that want to erupt, as with the womxn in the poem of Phạm Thị Ngọc Liên "I want to open my hands into the sky and scream" (title poem of the collection *I want to open my hands into the sky and scream*, Hội Nhà Văn publisher, 1992). But in their essence, these voices are still expressing a need for the personal and emotional safety of living in the arms of a man, which can be seen as an image of the limitations on gender, demarcated and approved by popular societal structures. This is precisely why the poetry of Dư Thị Hoàn—luminous highlights of womxn's poetry during the Renovation period, with its painful narrative of a young womxn's choice to be broken when a lover is careless with her body, emerged as a more shocking story: "After some gentle / Moments on a stone bench / You did not rebutton my dress" ("Broken", *Footpath*, 1988). I do not want to see this broken-heartedness merely as a passive circumstance, an acceptance, and endurance of pain,

After her two works *Lối nhỏ I Footpath (1988), and Bài mẫu giáo sáng thế I Early Songs of World Creation* (1993) had such resonance, she elected nearly private silence. In 2005, after twelve years, Dư Thị Hoàn announced she was preparing to publish a third collection of poetry *Du nữ ngâm I Lyrical Notes of a Lady Wanderer*, simultaneously revealing a novel *Truyền nhân của Rồng I The Dragon Successor* and collection of her travel writing, but until now (2018) these works have yet to be published.

nor as a womxn's pain nakedly exaggerated. I want to see here, rather, a choice to be ruptured, perhaps as a necessity that could not be otherwise, despite its extreme harshness. An ending that does not lead to a traditional marriage as in the smooth scripts from early times of "We will be husband and wife," but rather the poem can be read as the choice to detach from the male body in order to become an independent womxn. Feminine pride, perhaps itself a myth, can be asserted and at the same time, it can I must self-destruct in order extend the capabilities of its embrace. This poem once stirred a moral debate regarding behaviors in love and the taboos of poetry at that time. I look at the womxn in Dư Thị Hoàn's poetry, and the poetic being Dư Thị Hoàn herself as beings in labor, naked and aching, challenging the heavy pressures of history and fate with audacity, while being aware of the inevitable ruptures of becoming individuals. And at some point, the pent-up voices erupt from a cramped and buried and burning place, full of torment.

I do not think I can claim that a second or third wave of awakening feminism has been set in motion in Vietnamese literature with the womxn poets of the early part of the century whose work I analyzed above. But it is possible to see, step by step, that Vietnamese womxn poets, regardless of geography and generation, have expressed, shared, and sent echoes of their voices this way and that—voices which are gradually rising in strength, increasingly candid, more direct, less restrained, and more widely exposed. Exploitation of the bodily materials, at times overwhelming and thematically limited by methods of approach that must vigilantly care for the susceptibility of womxn's bodies to be rendered into tools, rendered into motifs of sexuality, or deliver overly simplified messages—can be seen as a natural consequence of the process of self-emancipation from the pressures of taboo, and, simultaneously, act as an effective strategy in the endeavors to reaffirm independence and oppose the patriarchal ideology and discourses that suppress womxn's physicality under sophisticated mechanisms.

I hold significant this lengthy and persistent process of transformation in how womxn reflect themselves: from the awareness of a suppressive situation to the awareness of a value, from criticizing a marginalized condition, debunking the current state of social and literary norms, attacking the oppressive messages of patriarchal social structures and masculine discourses that shape womxn with mythologized notions of femininity, beauty, love, sexuality, marriage, and so on, to a private self-reflection through the very structure of one's own body, thus opening the capacity to elevate the body's language, and from the act of referencing oneself inside a masculine framework to the effort of extricating oneself from that framework and becoming independent bodies. This is not a struggle that comes from nowhere and returns to nowhere, initiated by loose and wild womxn poets in order to violate taboos or demolish "fine customs, good habits." More, it is a struggle that carries a tiny hope inside the accumulated efforts of a collective resonant energy coming from single individuals who stand side by side, and which in some way connect to the ideas that Carol Hanish made famous in her notes originally titled *The Personal is Political* (1969): "There are no personal solutions at this time. There is only collective action for a collective solution."

By choosing to write, with the not-easy endurance accompanying that choice, by continuing with one's work and poetic existence, the voices of Vietnamese womxn poets embody sufferers, witnesses, fighters, and self-emancipators; together as one and synchronous with womxn's liberation movements around the world. And this effort is certainly still continuing, here, as well as wherever you are reading this from. I hope to revive, erase, and extend questions that have been dug up in Vietnamese literature, push farther, open wider the calls, emancipate literary experiments, and expand every sense of self-location in equality and in the resistance to patriarchy. I believe that the story of feminism and femininity is not necessarily the story of replicated patterns or limited frame-works, rather it's a story of perspectives, of concrete human touch and exchange. For me, being able to see the possibilities of free individual voices still brings trust and sharing to a place where poets truly possess a private space. Although tiny, that place brims with powerful permeability and resonance, strong and tender. Miên Đáng's "Tiny, Tiny" stands in for my dear love of this hard-won creation of visible privacy:

Tiny, Tiny

This tiny Private Space. I am also tiny.

This tiny book. I am also tiny.

This tiny mouse. I am also tiny.

This tiny hot breath. I am also tiny.

Tiny humans. I am also tiny.

Tiny you, tiny me.

Tiny lonely

whole earth dissolving into sweet noises that finish the 24th hour.

Peaceful sleep.

Work Cited

Dư Thị Hoàn." Broken." *Lôi Nhớ: Thơ.* ["Footpath."] Haiphong: Hội Văn Học Nghệ Thuật Hải Phòng, 1988.

Fraser, Nancy. "Rethinking the Public Sphere: A Contribution to the Critique of Actually Existing Democracy." *Social Text*, no. 25/26, Web. 1990. pp. 56–80. *JSTOR*, www.jstor.org/stable/466240.

Hanisch, Carol. The Personal is Political: The Women's Liberation Movement Classic with a New Explanatory Introduction. *Women of the World Unite: Writings by Carol Hanisch*. Web. 1969/2007. http://www.carolhanisch.org/CHwritings/PersonalisPol.pdf

Lê Thị Thấm Vân. "Giơ tay." ["Raise Your Hands If."] *Tiền Vệ*, Web. tienve.org/home/literature/viewLiterature.do?action=viewArt-work&artworkId=5206.

Lê Thị Thấm Vân. "Giá tự do." ["Freedom's Cost."] *Tiền Vệ*, Web. http://tienve.org/home/activities/viewTopics.do?action=viewArt-work&artworkId=1729

Lê, Thị Mây. "Vô đề". ["Titleless."] *Những mùa trăng mong chờ. [Seasons of awaiting moon]*. Sài Gòn: Giáo Dục Press, 1980. Print.

Lynh Bacardi. "Bẩm sinh." ["By Birth."] *Dự báo phi thời tiết [Forecast of Non-weather]*. Hà Nội: Hội Nhà Văn Press, 2006. Print.

Miên Đáng. "Nhỏ bé, nhỏ bé." ["Tiny, Tiny."] *Tiền Vệ*, Web. http://tienve.org/home/activities/viewTopics.do?action=viewArt-work&artworkId=1729

Nguyễn Thị Hoàng Bắc. "Nghinh hôn." ["Betrothal."] *26 Nhà Thơ Việt Nam Đương Đại. [26 Contemporary Vietnamese Poets]*. Edited by Đinh Trường Chinh, Phan Nhiên Hạo, Thận Nhiên, Đỗ Quyên, Nguyễn Đức Tùng, Westminster: Tân Thư, 2002. Print.

Nguyễn Thị Hoàng Bắc. "Ngọn cỏ." ["Tips of Grass."] *26 Nhà Thơ Việt Nam Đương Đại. [26 Contemporary Vietnamese Poets]*. Edited by Đinh Trường Chinh, Phan Nhiên Hạo, Thận Nhiên, Đỗ Quyên, Nguyễn Đức Tùng chủ trương. Westminster: Tân Thư, 2002. Print.

Nguyễn Trần Khuyên. "Một nền văn học xây dựng từ Đực và phục vụ cho Đực." ["A Literature Constructed by the Masculine and Serving the Masculine."] *Talawas*, Web. 4 July 2005. www.talawas.org/talaDB/showFile.php?res=4231&rb=0102

Nguyễn Trần Khuyên. "Chống văn chương miệt thị nữ giới."
["Against Misogynist Literature Campaign."] Petition. *Gió-O*, Web.
www.gio-o.com/NguyenTranKhuyenTalawas.html

Phạm Thị Ngọc Liên. *Em Muốn Giang Tay Giữa Trời Mà Hét: Thơ. [I
Want to Open My Hands into the Sky and Scream.]* Hà Nội: Hội nhà văn,
1992. Print.

Trần Minh Quân. "Hai đứa kinh nguyệt trần truồng." [Two Moonly
Ones in the Nude.] *Gió-O.*, Web. www.gio-o.com/Tran- MinhQuan-
4BaiTho.html

Open Mouth: The Revolt of Trash
translated by Nguyễn Hoàng Quyên

i plei poetry
sand bhụbbler krabs plei sand
kid$ plei other thïngs
— Bùi Chát

Poetic Citizens of Alley 47

My first encounter
with the Mở Miệng
(Open Mouth) group's
"filthy" poems that a
friend had printed from
literary web forums got
me thinking: was there
no other way of rebel-
lion besides malicious
mischief? Later, having
read and observed the

TN: Open Mouth poets
frequently play with corrupt
spellings and diacritics in
the original Vietnamese.
Throughout this essay, the
English translation inevitably
approximates and improvises
on their signature play.

group's practice, I gained different insights and found my ini-
tial serious sentiments laughable. I have since received their
latest poetry collections and revisited their earlier photocopied
publications, except for a couple that became untraceable after
multiple rounds of interrogation and document destruction
by the cultural security guards. I am interested in changes
among the group's members before and after the formation of
the name Mở Miệng. The six founding members, originally
literary friends at the Sài Gòn University of Social Sciences
and Humanities Class of 2001, consisted of Lý Đợi, Bùi Chát,
Khúc Duy, Nguyễn Quán, Hoàng Long, and Trần Văn Hiến
who self-published together the poetry collection *Vòng tròn
sáu mặt (Six-sided Circle)* in 2002. Hoàng Long and Trần Văn
Hiến soon afterwards left the group due to conflicting literary
philosophies. Shortly after the remaining four poets released
the collection *Mở Miệng* (published June 2002), Nguyễn Quán
withdrew from the group to become a monk and Khúc Duy sim-

ply disappeared from the scene once the collection *Hầm bà lằn* (*Smorgasbord*, 2004) was published. Over the last couple decades, besides releasing poetic works, Open Mouth, with two remaining members, Lý Đợi and Bùi Chát, has persistently pursued underground | independent publishing path. They founded Giấy Vụn (Scrap Paper Press), a highlight in Việt Nam's contemporary samizdat movement that resists censorship in the struggle for freedom of publication. In recent years, their reputation in publishing seems to have overshadowed their poetry, especially after Bùi Chát was awarded the 2011 Freedom to Publish Prize by the International Publishers Association (IPA) and has since been subject to frequent surveillance and interrogation by security agencies. To me, their persistent courage in self-publishing expresses a dimension in the poetic lives of individuals deemed unfit for order and discipline,

On April 25, 2011, at the 37th International Book Fair, Bùi Chát, as the co-founder of Giấy Vụn, was awarded the Freedom to Publish Prize by the IPA which was founded in 1896 to protect human rights and authors' rights, resist censorship, and honor the freedom to publish. Returning from the award ceremony, Bùi Chát was held at Tân Sơn Nhất airport for around 48 hours and got his laptop and passport confiscated along with the IPA's certificate and two bilingual poetry collections: Bài thơ một vần (Poem of a Single Rhyme) by Bùi Chát and Khi kẻ thù ta buồn ngủ (When Our Enemy Falls Asleep) by Lý Đợi, published by Eva Tass in 2010. The information was recounted by Bùi Chát.

which I respect. Certainly, the poetry of Open Mouth can't be fully perceived as autonomous from both their significant independent publishing practice and personal lives on the margin. Nevertheless, due to my penchant for poetic questions (as opposed to, say, an intentional evasion of other investigations), I do not aim for this essay to objectively and exhaustively identify this infamous group of poets. The consistent points of inquiry throughout my research remain: who are these Open Mouth poets? Is Open Mouth simply a dissident poetry group? What are the potentials of renovation and revolution in Open Mouth's practice, particularly their coup d'état in poetic material with the creation of lingo such as "Trash poetry," "Filthy poetry," or "Cemetery poetry," which have sparked multidirectional debates in various online spaces of the diaspora? How have their practices contributed to contemporary Vietnamese poetry movements or might they gradually fade as memories since Bùi Chát and Lý Đợi have lately grown more quiet as poets? These questions force me to keep my distance from the group's active and diverse participation in publishing and the arts in order to examine only their poetic manifesto and practice. The shape of Open Mouth, therefore, will be found in the language of poetry itself rather than the authors' social participation.

Before entering the main questions, I would like to revisit the past few years' discussions on Open Mouth's poetic manifesto and works to show how they once occupied the spotlight of the poetic stage. Below is the editor Đinh Tuấn Anh's riveting sketch of the poetic group who wreaked havoc on the literary scene in the early 2000s. The article was featured in the 2004 column "Young Sài Gòn Poetry" on the (now defunct) Vietnamese online literary journal *Evan*:

> There is a group of young writers who self-publish in the format of photocopies and consider them official documents. They roam the streets of Sài Gòn, through cafés, dog meat restaurants, day, night, streetlight, traffic, dust, noise. They make poetry. And short stories, novels, essays, performances, installations, conceptual art, and visual art. And they declare. Self-positioning, or more accurately, self-recognizing as part of the avant garde movements such as postmodernism, they push poetry into "dead ends," checkmating readers with renovated language. They willingly challenge other poets on the professionalism and academicism in

poetry; the challenge extends especially to, as Open Mouth bluntly point out, the conservative generation of poets who refuse to let go of their supposed forte. And of course, they are willing to be challenged.

Many still recall this episode in which Đinh Tuấn Anh, together with Trần Tiến Cao Đăng, as a "reward" for a particular column, were discharged from *Evan* in 2005, and the entirety of *Evan's* 2004-05 archived data was deleted. In 2005, as the cultural assistant of the Goethe Institute in Hà Nội, Đinh Tuấn Anh continued to organize a reading of Open Mouth's poetry at the institute (originally set for June 17, 2005), but the program was cancelled under a request from Việt Nam's Ministry of Culture. Open Mouth became a target under attack from mainstream media with articles such as "The Open Mouth Group with Trash Called Poetry" (Trúc Linh) and "There is a Black Channel in Vietnamese literature" (Hồng Cương)-articles which Open Mouth poets considered "not worthy of response" (Lý Đợi). To this day, mainstream news agencies and national presses still reject or censor articles on Open Mouth, except for overt condemnations of the group. Open Mouth has henceforth been labeled as marginal and taboo, causing even academics to keep their safe distance.

Prior to the founding of the group, Lý Đợi and Bùi Chát, along with other young poetic voices of Sài Gòn, had emerged with some acclaim. They were introduced and translated into English by Linh Dinh and featured in Vietnamese poetry anthologies abroad such as *26 Vietnamese Contemporary Poets* (Tân Thư Press, USA, 2001) and *An Anthology of New Form* (Tân Hình Thức Club, USA, 2006). In the realm of poetry, Open Mouth is perhaps more capacious than what primarily attracted the local and overseas media, a group of dissident poets.[7] Inrasara, a poet-critic in the Việt Nam Writers' Association, has long expressed an interest in this group and their poetry through his book introductions, reviews, and interviews, published on different media channels. The article "A Crisis among Sài Gòn's Young Poets," first published in *Tiền Vệ* (March 17, 2005) and later featured in the book *Dialogue with the New*, published in 2008, self-proclaimed to be "not at all edited, not even a word," has referenced Open Mouth in Sài Gòn's vibrant poetry during that period:

> Masked as extremist if not overzealous, the Open Mouth group and their poetic products resemble a "rotten breeze stirring the poetic atmosphere," an atmosphere that is currently motionless. [Open Mouth] is itself a crisis. It abruptly emerges and shocks us, pulling our attention towards the general crisis of Vietnamese poetry, a crisis that ought to be seen as a favorable sign.

Researcher Trần Ngọc Hiếu regards Open Mouth as those "who write with Nietzsche's hammer" and considers them a refreshing source of material for explorers invested in the provocative nature of literature. Simultaneously, in a series of academic articles,[8] he proposes several questions in theory and methodology on how to approach Vietnamese contemporary poetry.

Additionally, the passionate reception of critic Đoàn Cầm Thi[9] and support from poets and friends throughout Việt Nam and the diaspora such as Nguyễn Quốc Chánh, Linh Dinh, Đỗ Kh., Đặng Thân, Nguyễn Đăng Thường, Trần Wũ Khang, Như Huy,[10] Liêu Thái, etc. have stimulated the literary scene and formed a "minor myth" around Open Mouth, these hoodlum poets of Sài Gòn. The titles and catch phrases associated with them such as "citizens of alley 47," "Arhat Chamber," "photo[copy] publisher," "Filthy poetry," "Trash poetry," "resistant poetry," "poetic revolution," or "rotten breeze of poetry" have thus become infamous. In the opposite direction, notable articles by the poet Phan Nhiên Hạo[11] offered a cautionary stance against the atmosphere of exaltation that was threatening to dominate the discussion. His writings, however, ultimately "reheated the poetic pan" (Lý Đợi).

Nhã Thuyên

It can be said that Open Mouth's extremist declarations and compositions were a powerful nudge for the arguments and conflicts within and beyond poetry. Beyond literary implications, these exchanges revealed a sense of confinement and an urgent desire of local and diasporic writers to activate the climate of life and art in contemporary Việt Nam. On one hand, to the official media, Open Mouth's emerging activities disclosed the suffocating mechanics of cultural censorship and the increasingly heated tension between the official and the unofficial. On the other hand, as praised by comrades "in the same boat" who were similarly viewed as marginal, Open Mouth became a node of reflections on Vietnamese poetry, especially on issues such as renovation versus revolution, poetry versus politics, and purity versus vulgarity in poetry and postmodernism. The openness of cyberspace attracted multidirectional opinions ranging from critical arguments to extravagant claims, resulting in a rich inventory of information that could function as an important database for literary historians and cultural researchers. That was a part of the story around the research and criticism on Open Mouth. Amid the chaos of commendation and condemnation, I would like to bring forward an effort to repaint a poetic portrait of Open Mouth beyond ethical debates and reductive political positions.

Open Mouth Declares: "We Do Not Make Poetry"

The assault on poetic conventions is the core of Open Mouth's seemingly colloquial and improvisational manifesto, with Lý Đợi's article, "Poetry: We Do Not Make Poetry" (2004). Seen in a larger context, this statement points to a dialogue between the present and the past, a battle between the novelty of the avant-garde and the decay of the conservative, a proposal of poetry as anti-poetry that is certainly not an outlier in the history of poetry, an attempt to resist perceptions that have turned fixed and fossilized, an urge to speak that arises within a suppressed presence. After referencing a pastiche poem by Bùi Chát, Open Mouth invokes Dadaism as a source of inspiration:

We (young writers in Sài Gòn) call this rhetorical device *pastiche*, a combination of satirical imitation and assemblage. Recall the *collage* device of Dadaists with their cut-tear-paste and mixed media paintings. Also known as *coercion*. Thanh Tùng's poem has been coerced by Bùi Chát (the way Postmodernism *raped* Modernism). So what is creativity? Creativity lies at the threshold of the coercer and the coerced.

Poetry oftentimes is just a casual fight, a little humor, a shock of perception, even a joke among drunkards, no less frivolous. [...] We do not make something too high-end, too uncouth or too eccentric, because we maintain that besides popular media's aesthetics, there has been/is a different kind of poetry—our poetry/our aesthetics, the aesthetics of those absorbed in making poetry, not critics or ethicists, moralists or sociologists.

   —"Poetry: We Do Not Make Poetry," Lý Đợi

In this manifesto, when using the phrase "poetic practice," Open Mouth's anti-poetic will to exist as an Other is manifest in multiple aspects including: i) the anti-poetic material—the poets do not hesitate "before topics rated as alien or vulgar by Vietnamese aesthetic traditions," ii) the anti-poetic act of not-making-poetry, which proposes a different relationship between the poet, the material, and the poetry; iii) the statement about belonging to the underground: "our poetry is not subject to the editorial screen of publishing houses." Anti-poetry is a double protest: not only opposing tradition, which they consider synonymous with archaic aesthetics, Open Mouth also protests the school of poetry that works exclusively with *words* and *meanings* through experiments encased within linguistic units. Open Mouth poets propose poetry-making as an *act*. The entire being of the poet with gestures and environments makes poems that no longer exist in isolation, but rather embody links in an endless chain of interactions. Refusing to simply churn out new poems, Open Mouth declares, destroys, and proposes, persistently pursuing the project of decentering poetry from the poetic conventions that have reigned for millennia in a country

Nhã Thuyên

where poetry is traditionally sacralized with heroic missions to "carry the Tao," "speak the will," or "preserve the heritage."

I believe Open Mouth's combative proposal of poetry as a conceptual art practice should not be regarded as an imitation of imported fashions or an arbitrary mutation in the so-called Vietnamese poetic tradition, but rather, as a desire to protest from within. Unwilling to dwell in shadows, the marginalized begins to question the notion of revolution and the ones who claim to revolutionize poetry; they question the very label of "the unofficial" itself, a label imposed on them as if to brand a peculiar sort of food that requires caution. With their decla- ration, Open Mouth fulfills the verdict of Otherness by their signature poetic practices: "Trash poetry," "Filthy poetry," "Cemetery poetry." Conceptually, these practices have been inspired by the trash and filthy artistic movements of the world, letting them precipitate into an insurgent attitude of destruc- tion and mockery: the literary past is an infinite landfill where they freely dive, scavenge, and indulge in ostensibly filthy, extremist, and obscene materials, unfazed by the risk of stum- bling on mines.

In the reconfiguration of poetic concepts and practices, the negating word "not" (in "we do not make poetry") is the space of free play in both language and consciousness. Similar to the addition of the prefix "post-" before "ism", the work of decentering and redefining poetic conceptions continues without end. At the creative and critical foundation of institutions, what must be demolished is the coordinate system that projects what qualifies or fails as poetry onto empty abstract metaphysics. Only then would open possibilities of reading and writing unsettle the lives of poetry and its participants who might otherwise be stuck in blocks or live with their creative delusions. Each poet, while making poems, should be summoning possibilities of (making) poetry. To trace the origin of poetic concepts is impossible and meaningless; the poetry-making subject endlessly pursues ever-slippery concepts in a thrilling race that blurs the distinction between the Playful and the Real, between Making and Unmaking, between seriousness and nonsense—perhaps an inescapable game of chase.

Image 4: Four members of Open Mouth, 2006. From left to right: Bùi Chát, Khúc Duy, Lý Đợi, Nguyễn Quán. Image courtesy © Open Mouth.

Nhã Thuyên

Open Mouth Plei Poetry: "Pardon Me, Can't Stand It"

TN: *Xaùo choän chong ngaøy* mutates from the standard spelling of *Xáo trộn trong ngày*, meaning daily upheavals.

"thơ jác từ jưởi" is a distortion of "thơ rác từ rưởi" ("rubbish poetry from refuse").

The title "Hỏa/mù/mờ" works due to the monosyllabic structure of Vietnamese which supports mischievous reassemblage. The breakdown and re-combination of 'hỏa mù' (smoke screen) and 'mù mờ' (murky) produce a sum of total chaos.

"Trash poetry" and "Filthy poetry" are concepts proposed by Bùi Chát, starting with his 2003 collection *Xaùo choän chong ngaøy (Däily ùpheavalɔ)* which featured the slogan "jubbish poetry from jefuse" ("thơ jác từ jưởi"). He continued in the same direction with "Cemetery poetry," a term self-coined in the collection *Xin lỗi, chịu hổng nổi (Parɔon me, can't ɔtanɔ it,* 2007), with the introduction titled "Ablaze/Foggy/Opaque" ("Hỏa/Mù/Mờ") by Bùi Chát. I would like to cite the segment in its entirety, preserving the author's own grammar rules:

After an almost two-year-long break from all literary and publishing activities due to health reasons, since early August, I have launched a project called "Got dis use dis got dat use dat" ("Có jì dùng jì có nấy dùng nấy"): a sidewalk poetry project that aims to publish an anthology featuring 47 authors and many other individual works. For the project, I revisited old manuscripts and stumbled upon: Pardon me, can't stand it.

Parɔon me, can't ɔtanɔ it was originally volume 1 of *The Mummy Returnɔ*, the collection of 333 cemetery poems completed in 2004 which, for reasons incomprehensible to myself, has not yet been published (by me). This cemetery poetry collection is a significant part of *Made in Vietnam*, a controversial work of conceptual art.

My job is simply to extract one part of one portion of one complete project in order to form one part of one portion of one other to-be-completed project as I, the author, execute part two, "Got dis use dis got dat use dat." This step is identical to that of taking a complete poem by somebody else and turning it into a (potentially) incomplete poem of mine.

The goal is for the poetry collection to return to its right place & role: cemetery goods.

Why must I do that? There are certainly many responses to such a question, but first and foremost: no organization or individual have coerced or cajoled/bribed me. I only want to execute my own mandate of the past few years: Try not to make anything new, if possible: One should reuse what has been/is available.

(Is it not less work that way?)

Finally, this collection is an inseparable component of trash poetry and trash art, which have constituted Open Mouth's most controversial issues over the past few years. The conscious and thorough practice of cemetery–trash poetry, in my humble opinion, has transformed Open Mouth artists and those sharing the same philosophy into authors with (perhaps) the most vivid flavors of tradition throughout Việt Nam's cultural/literary history.

A cultural/literary history of trash.

—"Ablaze/Foggy/Opaque" ("Hỏa/Mù/Mờ"), Bùi Chát

Most poems in *Däily ùpheavals* resemble ribald folk tales of trivial objects that seemingly mean nothing as they exist only in the vernacular, an underground world where stories may feature a single broomstick, women as mice in the sewer, panties, a bowl, a couple hairs, a few farts, copulation, and many other lewd matters.

Not long after, Bùi Chát dedicated an entire collection to the "concept" of cursing, *Cái lồn bỏ đi và những bài thơ chửi [bới, lộn]* *(The Cunt that Got Away and Poems of Cursing [Cursing-meddling, Cursing-tumbling])*, which explores the ferocious intensity of colloquial ribald language. Bùi Chát thoroughly practices plurilingualism, using puns that complicate translation and various manners of shape-shifting: distorting sentence structures, inverting spelling standards, morphing urban and officialized language, imitating speech dialects of the rural North (where Thái Bình province, Bùi Chát's hometown, exemplifies a dialect deemed "defective" by the rules of "correct" standardized Vietnamese), and other local dialects that have barely survived in ribald folk tales.

Demotic tongues are not only taboo among contemporary writings but also estranged from the Việt Nam's previously avant-garde word-laborers dedicated exclusively to the shadows of words and ways of creating rhythm. Chasing after aesthetic and exotic verses, they came to be known as poets of *the school of letters (dòng chữ)*, a term coined by the poet Hoàng Hưng to describe a renovation trend practiced by Northern Vietnamese poets such as Lê Đạt and Dương Tường who, in pursuit of mellifluous syllables and sounds, deviated from the dominant *school of meaning (dòng nghĩa)* in Vietnamese poetry. In the case of Open Mouth, romantic lyricism is destroyed as the poetic subject looks into a convex mirror and sees a self-translated portrait of a hypertrophic, distorted, and worldly underdog. Inserting the vulgar into his poetry, Bùi Chát does not provoke or, more accurately, he does not curse for the sake of being provocative. He uses words as egalitarian materials where poetry is no longer reserved solely for sophisticated letters and where overbearing humans who mistake language for a numb instrument might end up dethroned and ousted by the words themselves. Nonconformity—what poets often strive to attain—lies in life, a fact Bùi Chát discovered and turned into a poetic rule, which has in turn revealed different angles of poetry-making in an engagement with vernacular language and reality.

The poem's title could be pronounced as vô địt ("no fuck") in certain Northern dialects.

champion

a mediocre cock, he treasures, modeling the forefathers
to protect, to cherish–allowing no fault
he hardens and suffers despite the desire to f-
launt his cockity

vowing virginity to the end, though girls do follow
thanks to moral virtues. each day he looks in the mirror,
wrapping a cloth
around the groin [seriously] many times to possess...
a prepared future
each cunt that got away like a small rivulet
he does not know the [damned] forefathers dead before
his birth
lived half their lives uncaressed, he has touched nobody
still... intact & black

for some old age solace. he stealthily moves
the cock to the back and thrusts it in the ass

[sob sob]

TN: Ba Giai, Tú Xuất and Thủ Thiệm were non-fictive 19th-century figures who became archetypal storytellers in the Vietnamese tradition of satirical folk tales.

In the attempt to exterminate lyricism, accomplish surface description, and utilize the vulgar, not all Open Mouth authors have gained the same level of success. Khúc Duy, with his smorgasbord of profanities in *Smorgasbord* (2003), a collection in the vein of the "continually crass," turned out to be a mere vent of meaninglessness and ennui. Bùi Chát blasphemes like a folk storyteller, like Ba Giai, Tú Xuất, and

Thủ Thiệm, like a poetry promoter for eardrums fed up with the refined sounds. Lý Đợi extracts various poetic materials from colloquial journalism, reconfiguring journalistic texts, and bringing poetry closer to slogan and slogan regurgitation. The poets have created a flea market of authentic local brands mixed with smuggled items. I suppose, Open Mouth's first and foremost contribution in the practice of "filthy poetry" is their decanonization of aesthetic conventions around "noble" and "literary" language whose inertia has become a creative block for poetry-making in Việt Nam. Open Mouth has thus proposed a new set of communication rules around poetic language and material. Their contribution lies not in the use of profanity but the carnivalesque spirit or the public-poetry quality, which brings poetry closer to daily behavior and folk custom. The argument for the openly in[discriminate]nocent usage of vocabulary that references sexual organs and relations such as "cunt," "cock," or "fuck" is an attempt to re-establish textual equality, which possesses a powerful appeal in its subversive intent.

In fact, in Việt Nam, the political use of profane language might also suggest a life attitude. Obscene literature, often suppressed and excluded, seeks refuge in the folk undercurrent of rural opera, ribald tales, and proverbial songs. In an effort to claim their voices, many poets have used the vulgar to unchain and overturn the taboo by expressing political anguish or sexual liberation. The poet Nguyễn Quốc Chánh considers the vulgar as "transmutations of political obsessions on the body," and as ways of "spitting at deceptive propaganda." He says, "wherever human beings are robbed of their freedom of speech, whatever useful means of resistant literature could be reasonably selected since this is a non-theoretical space." The critic Nguyễn Hưng Quốc in an essay titled "Và các thứ con khác" ("And other animal kinds", *Tiền Vệ*, 2003) has asserted, "In a place like Việt Nam, perhaps only saints would abstain from cursing."

Open Mouth's conscious infliction, via "filthy" material and words, constitutes only one of the many linguistic reactions in Vietnamese contemporary poetry, yet it has produced mayhem partly because the group's practices transgress the boundaries of preexisting aesthetic standards; they shock, both visually and psychologically; they make use of common material and yet face backlash for acts marked as taboo. And whenever taboo resurfaces, so too does the inevitable question of artistic freedom: is there a limit to this freedom? Is it we who ought to gradually erase the entrenched taboos within ourselves? As "Filthy poetry" overwhelms our common aesthetic threshold, it might prompt us to suspect the poems' salacious language and the poets' supposed lack of discipline. Using the obscene as a way to deal with text and a vessel for an iconoclastic voyage, Open Mouth has somewhat overcome the struggle to speak. However, the bristling repetition of vulgar vocabulary tends to foreclose other pathways. The "anti-poetic" conquers and inherits the crown, causing the initial creativity to turn into lethargy and become a new obstructive force. The idealistic conception of equality for poetic material and language ironically gives rise to an energy of destruction instead of rebirth. My perhaps redundant question remains: where could the filthy face and body take poetry?

In addition to "Filthy poetry," Open Mouth's specialties also include "Trash poetry" coupled with the device of pastiche. The tactic has instigated controversy especially when the authors not only lampoon their own materials (e.g. Bùi Chát made remixes and parodies of his own poems in *Däily ùpheavals*) but cook up poetry using ready-made and well-known poems the way Marcel Duchamp appropriated the Mona Lisa or Andy Warhol reworked the image of Marilyn Monroe. In *Pardon me, can't stand it*, among many other famous poems, *Chọn (The Choice)* by Văn Cao is transformed into a new work that offers a new interpretation of the original poem.

Nhã Thuyên

The Choice of Văn Cao

Between life and death
He chooses life
To preserve life
He chooses death

That is all [the end]

Ingredient: *The Choice* by Văn Cao

This original poem, often associated with the tragedy of
choice or the desire for aesthetic life and sublime ascension,
has generated comedy out of its own seriousness, especially if
we bear in mind Văn Cao's life. A biographical note of Văn
Cao's tragic life might be helpful here. Văn Cao (1923-1995)
authored Việt Nam's official national anthem, *Tiến quân ca
(Marching Song)*, and was one of most well-recognized faces in
Vietnamese modern music. Among the sufferers of *Nhân Văn-
Giai Phẩm* affair, Văn Cao was banned from writing for several
decades. During his lifetime, only one poetry collection was
published under the title *Lá* (*Leaf*, New Work Press, 1988).
Adding the few words "That is all [the end]" as a viewer's
commentary at the end of a tragicomic play, Bùi Chát satirizes
the idealism of ascent metaphors in Vietnamese poetry and its
excessively grave language which, in his vision, should by now
be buried and consigned to oblivion. Using the rhetoric of folk
ribaldry, propaganda poetry,
graffiti poetry, Bamboo Pen
poetry, and slogan poetry,
Bùi Chát pulls conventional
paradigms out of their ele-
vated standing, dragging
them down to the worldly
realm of unmetaphysical and

Bút Tre (Bamboo Pen) was
a 20th-century Vietnamese
poet's pseudonym and the
style of popular folk poetry
named after him.

unphilosophical language where delight, laughter, and release
come with startling self-reflections and awakenings. Here, the
free play with poetic language by adding, cutting, assembling,

and impishly remixing ready-made materials, hence the formation of Bùi Chát's new infamous poems, does not erase but co-exist with the original poems and intensify intertextual dynamics. This is why, despite its simplicity, applicability, and mass reproducibility, Bùi Chát's textual play is a critical landmark as it attacks and redefines what threatens to become institutionalized truths.

Lý Đợi's pastiche, on the other hand, is executed mostly using trash materials found in Vietnamese daily news and explicitly socio-political Eastern European poems translated into Vietnamese and published on literary web magazines by diasporic poet-translators such as Hoàng Ngọc Biên and Diễm Châu. Playing with Vietnamese local contexts, Lý Đợi both translates and implants texts, sometimes even importing wholesale Eastern European contexts to create a sociocultural hodgepodge that travels across space and time. To take one page, Lý Đợi's poem "Hiện thực xã hội chủ nghĩa" ("Socialist Realism") is rooted in Ryszard Krynicki's *Socialist Realism* (translated into Vietnamese by Hoàng Ngọc Biên in Tiền Vệ). Lý Đợi rearranges and juxtaposes originals lines with newly added details:

The ghost is a dove of peace
The corpse is a plate of party snacks
With a small bottle of white rice wine, a red bottle
The white flag – planted in the center of the beak
Fiddled back and forth
Sitting down standing up
By the ice cream seller
serene afternoon
along the yellow plaster wall
in alley 47
several eavesdroppers
snake-like faces
unable to bite
how bitter

The poem "Mới khai quật bản sắc văn hoá Việt Nam" ("Recent Excavation of Vietnamese Identity") offers another pattern of the contemporary folk genre, which has its origin in a *talaCu*—the humor supplement of *Talawas*—issue published in December 2005. A humorous story reports that a peasant from Thanh Hóa has discovered the Vietnamese cultural identity while digging a fishpond. Mr. Cù ["Cù" meaning "to tickle" in Vietnamese], the peasant protagonist, proclaims, "We were digging about five meters deep when we came upon a strange object. When my brothers and I hauled it up, I immediately suspected it was the Vietnamese identity because I thought it looked very weird."

However, the poem's concluding commentary seems to significantly diminish the humor of this poetic-folk story:

> Vietnamese cultural identity
> It looks like a rotting cadaver
> Like an old pillow
> Like a pus-filled wound
> Hauled from the sludge
> Reeking of death…

Here, as the boundary is blurred between the primary text and the secondary, between the translated and the re-translated, the hunt for the origin again proves to be futile. Lý Đợi consumes poetry and is willing to let poetry dissipate the way we consume daily news. I presume, when translated into another language and uprooted from the Vietnamese vernacular, Lý Đợi's poems lose much of their humor and satirical meaning. The poems are most animate and organic when read by the author himself in his hometown cadence of Điện Bàn (Quảng Nam province) to which I have had the chance to listen at the famous Arhat Chamber of Open Mouth poets in Sài Gòn.

It has been commonly suggested that Open Mouth's use of pastiche as a rhetorical device and political disposition offers nothing original since the readymade art movement of repurposing old material and reconfiguring past masterpieces has become a cliché. Might "Cemetery poetry" be dead? Is Dada indeed gone? I imagine that art movements, once they have ceased in a certain context, could enter rebirth in another. The value of Open Mouth's poetic texts or their inventive edge compared to the primary texts lies in their capacious interaction with context and intertextuality—"text" here is understood as social-political-cultural texts. When the text is inherently intertextual, it should no longer be evaluated as a complete work in which words bear the mission to carry value, but rather an infinitely unfolding cultural reaction across different contexts, spaces, and reading movements. Certainly, the peril of imitation is invariably latent in each creative effort. Especially in cyberspace, the imitation of new-found devices becomes so dangerously facile it risks becoming falsehood, and therefore the lifetime of a fresh device might be terribly brief. Between superficial and substantial renovation is often a mere tenuous crease.

Image 5: A sample of Open Mouth's poetry collections published by Giấy Vụn Press

The practice of "Trash poetry" and "Trash art" was widely shared and spread in Vietnamese contemporary art and literature in multiple manners. The diasporic poet Nguyễn Đăng Thường had previously self-registered his copyright of a Vietnamese non-poetry poetry genre in which he uses negative prefixes as a way to concoct new poetry from pre-existing works. Phan Bá Thọ self-published a collection titled *Đống rác vô tận (Endless Pile of Trash)*. Nguyễn Quốc Chánh, in an interview by Lý Đợi, responded:

> My poetry certainly belongs to the tradition of trash. Because Việt Nam is a trash can of both the east and west. Over a thousand years of struggling and sleeping with Chinese, Western, Japanese, American and Russian empires, Việt Nam has acquired a uniquely tragic fate, both coquettish and noble, identical to the life of Ms. Kiều [...] The bickerings between the old and the new, between tradition and renovation, ultimately are inner (nội) affairs—
>
> TN: Inner bài, as in Nội bài, references the largest airport in Việt Nam, located in Hà Nội.
>
> innerwars/mongolia/furniture/chores/*bài* between two eastern and western filaments of trash. In this cultural milieu where pig trotters stand in for dog meat, my solution is: consume and dispose as quickly as possible these fresh strands of trash, both eastern (heresy) and western (venom).

In the vein of trash art, a 2010 controversial exhibition titled *Xà bần (Debris)*, a component of the *Concrete Cutting and Drilling* project, gathered a number of painters and artists around Ngô Lực's painting studio with the shared idea of creating a "no curator, no manifesto" space and "exhibiting only conceptual trash." These artists' effort to decenter artistic behavior and space counteracts the top-down approach of highly intellectualized and alienating spaces like foreign cultural centers and opulent galleries. The exhibition does not evoke beauty, and, thus, what normally passes as aesthetics becomes questionable. The event, at the very least, signals a wriggling resistance against repressive systems of control, especially invisible mechanisms perpetuated by knowledge systems that possess the power to name and label the Other. Certainly, unresolved questions linger on, concerning what generates visual allure, what makes certain works haunting or what constitutes the relationship between art and politics in "Trash poetry" and "Trash art."

Image 6: An installation view of the exhibition Debris, Ngô Lực's painting studio, Sài Gòn, 2010. Image courtesy of Ngô Lực.

Returning to Open Mouth's practice of "Trash poetry," "Filthy poetry," and "Cemetery poetry," the poets have caused a ruckus for conventional poetic methods and materials. They have destabilized or, at the very least, forced readers to reflect on the secure rank of poeticized language in nice-looking letters, metaphors, rhetorical devices, and renovation efforts that exclusively hinge on "pure" language. Open Mouth's revolution in language should not be defined as an establishment of a new canon; it is essential for the enrichment of Vietnamese literary language and the demolition of winsome things masqueraded as poetry.

Open Mouth, Once More

My entire analysis of Open Mouth's practice, ranging from their manifesto to their practice of "Trash," "Filthy," and "Cemetery" poetry, with a special focus on the early phase, is an effort to reconstruct a picture of Open Mouth as a poetry group. The core question therefore concerns their survival strategy as poetry practitioners and not as a sociocultural group of agitators whom Vietnamese authorities have labeled "dissidents." A couple of ajar questions on the innovative and revolutionary quality of their poetry practices might, however, extend the conversation on their potential. Might the poets continue their individual journeys or "is that all [the end]"?

With these questions in mind, I would be remiss to overlook a significant body of works by Open Mouth, which could be seen as their transition from thriving trash into explicitly socio-political poetry, a hazardous species of taboo in Việt Nam. Reacting against a corrupt and volatile society, the works of this period indeed positioned themselves in the stream of Vietnamese dissident poetry. Many poems by Bùi Chát, Lý Đợi, and Khúc Duy during this period revolved around the 2005 cancellation of their reading at the Goethe Institute, the police interrogations and the poets' relevant correspondences and discussions of the regime. In the collection Khi kẻ thù ta buồn ngủ (*When Our Enemy Falls Asleep*, 2009), Lý Đợi vehemently exhibits journalistic qualities in his streak of "consumerist poetry," which offers social and cultural commentaries. In the collection *Bài thơ một vần* (*A Poem of Single Rhyme*, 2010), in which the "single rhyme" revolves around the keyword "communism," Bùi Chát uncovers his ambition to overthrow the language of ideology with its propagandist slogans and chronic delusions. The following excerpt of the poem "Thói" ("Habits") by Bùi Chát, through a series of imperative sentences, bears the entrenched paradoxes of human society:

> —Sirs please let us know the truth!
> —Sirs please let us sleep with our wives/husbands!
> —Sirs please let us breathe!
> —Sirs please let us have justice in court!
> —Sirs please let us think differently!
> —Sirs please let us combat corruption!
> —Sirs please let us have free speech!
> —Sirs please let us congregate on the sidewalk!
> —Sirs please let us write this poem! ....

In my personal view, these poems' directly political content perhaps no longer shares the same exploratory path with Open Mouth's earlier "Trash," "Filthy," and "Cemetery" poetry. Associated with topical media manipulations and the latest political scandals or conspiracies, these works might easily turn into propaganda in their overzealous anti-propaganda. Their political implications are easily misunderstood or co-opted, and therefore, considered threatening: the cultural police's "engagement" with Open Mouth could be regarded as both creative repression and governmental precaution against "political acts disguised as literature." As a bleak result of a past long saturated with poetry strictly serving politics, the term "political poetry" in Việt Nam today continues to rely on a severely narrow, literal, and ideological definition of politics. As literary discourses become mere word play and the social function of literature comes under suspicion, the rise of Open Mouth's explicitly political poems seems to reduce not only the aesthetics but the resonant politics of the group's earlier period.

Open Mouth's most significant achievement, I would argue, is their aggressive all-out war on conventional poetic material, a militant operation that has unraveled important questions on the fate of language—which doubles as the fate of human beings—in a cultural and political milieu. It is also with this operation that Open Mouth's presence has become a text larger than linguistic texts as a result and reflection of Việt Nam's particular social context—a space of fury and anxiety with stringent cultural policies and underground angst, an apt milieu for rebellion, chaos, and nihilism. The choice to annihilate personal poetics in exchange for a different conception of poetry-making as a participatory act is, for me, Open Mouth's most poetic expression. In a way, these poets have sacrificed their personal breakthrough potential for their vision of a collective practice. It is Open Mouth's violent collision with and emancipation from the rigid order of poetic language and material, rather than their social declarations or commentaries, that made Open Mouth's aesthetical resistance (or resistant aesthetics). Such unique politics, in turn, has provided the necessary conditions for, if not wholly become, the pioneering quality of their practice.

Although I wouldn't regard Open Mouth as the representative of a generation, for the past couple decades they have remained a robust and prominent voice that fervently calls for the demolition of authoritarian fortresses in Vietnamese literature, namely, the visible wall of conspicuous censorship bureaus and invisible routines of making and reading poetry that hover like truth-preserving institutions in the language of ideology. Open Mouth forces us, the readers in Việt Nam, to resist getting drunkenly caught up in anarchy and take a sober look at the surrounding chaos, a space where all beings seem to be thrashing about, agitating for disruption, entertaining ridicule, facing confrontation, and crying out for a rupture in normalized values to unbolt possibilities of literary play. The language of artistic refusal often embodies a generative virtue, especially as the past turns into dubious debris and the present, blazing disorder. And so, even as fleeting fantasies of breakthrough and metamorphosis crumble with chimerical visions of a new canon, even as changes here lead to congestions elsewhere, the refusal has opened up vital dreams and substantial thoughts. Disobedience bears its own import, perhaps demanding no utterance of apology or interpretation.

Work Cited

Bùi Chát. "Hỏa/Mù/Mờ" ["Ablaze/Foggy/Opaque."] *Xin lỗi, chịu hổng nổi. [Pardon me, can't stand it]*. Sài Gòn: Giấy Vụn Press, 2007. Print.

Bùi Chát. "vô địch" ["Champion."] *Cái lồn bỏ đi và những bài thơ chửi [bới, lộn] [The Cunt that Got Away and Poems of Cursing [cursing-meddling, cursing-tumbling]*. Sài Gòn: Giấy Vụn Press, 2004. Print.

Bùi Chát. "Chọn lựa của Văn Cao." ["The Choice of Văn Cao."] *Xin lỗi, chịu hổng nổi. [Pardon me, can't stand it.]* Sài Gòn: Giấy Vụn Press, 2007. Print.

Bùi Chát. "Thói." ["Habits."] *Bài thơ một vần. [Single-rhyme Poems.]* Sài Gòn: Giấy Vụn Press, 2010. Print.

Đoàn Cầm Thi. "Về khoan cắt bê tông." ["On Concrete Cutting and Drilling".] *Talawas*, Web. 11 November 2005. http://www.talawas. org/talaDB/showFile.php?res=5759&rb=0101

Đoàn Cầm Thi. "Lại khoan cắt bê tông." ["Again, Concrete Cutting and Drilling".] *Talawas*, Web. 23 Dec. 2005. http://www.talawas.org/ talaDB/showFile.php?res=6109&rb=0101

Đoàn Cầm Thi. "Ta, một công dân ô nhục bậc nhất, một thánh nhân nát rượu…" — Thơ và Lề trong xã hội Việt Nam đương đại." ["I, an ignominious citizen, an alcoholic genie' – Poetry and Marginality in Contemporary Việt Nam."] *Tiền Vệ*, Web. 2005. http://www.tienve. org/home/activities/viewWorkOfTheMonth.do?action=viewArt-work&artworkId=5898

Đoàn Cầm Thi. "Một nền thơ mới Việt Nam: Sự xuất hiện một dòng thơ mới tại Sài Gòn." ["A New Vietnamese Poetry: The Emergence of a New Poetic Genre in Sài Gòn."] *Tiền Vệ*, Web. 15 Feb. 2006. http:// www.tienve.org/home/literature/viewLiterature.do?action=viewArt-work&artworkId=4448

Đoàn Cầm Thi. "Đoàn kết, đoàn kết, đại đoàn kết." ["Solidarity, Sol-idarity, Great Solidarity."] *Tiền Vệ*, Web. 22 Feb. 2006. www.tienve. org/home/literature/viewLiterature.do?action=viewArtwork&art-workId=4467

Đinh Tuấn Anh. "Thơ trẻ Sài Gòn." ["Young Sài Gòn Poetry."]. *Evan*, (website now closed), 2004.

Nhã Thuyên

Đỗ Lê Anhdao. "Open Mouth [Mo Mieng]: Begins a new history in Vietnamese Literature." *Nhà Magazine*, May-June 2005.

Hoàng Hưng. "Ngoảnh lại 15 năm." ["15 Years in Retrospect."] *Talawas*, Web. 12 June 2004. http://www.talawas.org/talaDB/showFile. php?res=2170&rb=0101

Hồng Cương. "Có một nhánh kênh đen trong dòng văn học Việt Nam." ["There is a Black Channel in   Vietnamese Literature."] *Hồ Chí Minh People's Police*, March 18, 2006.

Inrasara. "Song thoại với cái mới." ["Dialogue with the New."]. *Hà Nội Writers' Association*, 2008.

Khánh Hào. "Mở Miệng & Hip Hop." ["Open Mouth & Hip Hop."] *Nhà Magazine*, Jan-Feb 2005.

Lý Đợi. "Bốn lý do để xem bài viết của Trúc Linh là không đáng trả lời." ["Four Reasons Why Trúc Linh's Article is Not Worth Responding To."] *Talawas*, Web. 26 Dec 6, 2005. http://www.talawas.org/talaDB/suche.php?res=6120&rb=0101

Lý Đợi. "Thơ và chúng tôi không làm thơ." ["Poetry: We Do Not Make Poetry."] *Talawas*, Web. 16 Apr 2004. http://www.talawas.org/talaDB/showFile.php?res=1589&rb=0306

Lý Đợi. "Mới khai quật bản sắc văn hoá Việt Nam." ["Recent Excavation of Vietnamese Identity."] *When Our Enemy Falls Asleep: Khi Kẻ Thù Ta Buồn Ngủ. S.l.*: Eva Tas Foundation, 2010. Print.

Nguyễn Như Huy. "Tản mạn đôi chút với bài thơ Vô địch của Bùi Chát." ["Few Digressions on the Poem 'Champion' by Bùi Chát."] *Talawas*, Web. 21 Jan 2004. www.talawas.org/talaDB/showFile.php?res=386&rb=0103

Nguyễn Như Huy. "Vài nhận định về nhóm Mở Miệng." ["Several Opinions Regarding the Open Mouth Group."] *Talawas*, Web. 2005. http://vanchuongplusvn.blogspot.com/2013/07/inrasara-vai-nhaninh- ve-nhom-mo-mieng.html

Nguyễn Quốc Chánh, Lý Đợi."Thơ là (thờ ơ) khoét cho cái nhục (nhã, dục, vương) bốc mùi." ["Poetry is to (Poetically-Indifferently] Gouge a Hole through which the Humiliation (e.g. Shame, Lust, Disgraced Kings) Stinks.") *Talawas*, Web. July 26, 2004. talawas.org/talaDB/showFile.php?res=2479&rb=0102

Nguyễn Quốc Chánh, Trịnh Cung, Phan Nhiên Hạo, Chân Phương, Nguyễn Viện, Trần Vũ. "Văn chương hôm nay nhìn từ ngoài lề." ["Literature Today Viewed from the Margins."]. *LitViet*, Web. 29 Aug 2009. litviet.wordpress.com/2009/08/29/nguy%E1%B-B%85n-qu%E1%BB%91c-chanh-tr%E1%BB%8Bnh-cung-phan-nhien-h%E1%BA%A1o-chan-ph%C6%B0%C6%A1ng-nguy%E1%BB%85n-vi%E1%BB%87n-tr%E1%BA%A7n-vu-van--ch%C6%B0%C6%A1ng-hom-nay-nhin-t%E1%BB%AB-ngoai/

Nguyễn Hưng Quốc. "Và các thứ con khác." ["And Other Animal Kinds."] *Tiền Vệ*, Web. 2003. www.tienve.org/home/authors/viewAuthors.do?action=show&authorId=2

Nguyễn Như Huy. "Tản mạn đôi chút về bài thơ 'Vô Địch' của Bùi Chát." ["Few Digressions on the poem 'Champion' by Bùi Chát."] *Talawas*, Web. 21 Jan 2004.

Nguyễn Như Huy. "Vài nhận định về nhóm Mở Miệng." ["Several Opinions Regarding the Open Mouth Group."] *Talawas*, Web. 2005. vanchuongplusvn.blogspot.com/2013/07/inrasara-vai-nhan-inh-ve-nhom-mo-mieng.html

Phan Nhiên Hạo. "Thơ trẻ không nhất thiết phải là 'làn gió thối'." ["Young Poets Are Not Necessarily a Rotten Breeze."] *Talawas*, Web. 29 December 2003. www.talawas.org/talaDB/showFile.php?res=379&rb=07

—."Ba (khẩu) phần." ("Three (Oral) Portions.") *Talawas*, Web. 3 June 2004. www.talawas.org/talaDB/showFile.php?res=1646&rb=0102

—."Mới – Cũ trong thơ và Hậu hiện đại." ["The New and Old in Poetry and Postmodernism."] *Talawas*, Web. 21 May 2004. http://www.talawas.org/talaDB/showFile.php?res=1634&rb=0101

—."Nhà văn thế hệ sau chiến tranh và ông vua cởi truồng." ["Postwar Writers and the Pantless Emperor."] *Talawas*, Web. 24 February 2004. www.talawas.org/talaDB/showFile.php?res=416&rb=0401

—."Trao đổi với Đoàn Cầm Thi về… rác." ["A Dialogue with Đoàn Cầm Thi on… Trash."] *Talawas*, Web. 21 February 2006. www.talawas.org/talaDB/showFile.php?res=6497&rb=0101

Nga Phạm. "Việt Nam's Rude Poetry Delights Intelligentsia." *BBC Việt Nam*, Web. 31 August 2004. news.bbc.co.uk/2/hi/asia-pacific/3614760.stm

Nhã Thuyên

Pomonti, Jean-Claude. "Thư từ thành phố Hồ Chí Minh: Thơ không biên giới." ["Letter from Hồ Chí Minh City: Poetry Without Borders."] Translated into Vietnamese by Phan Bình. *Tiền Vệ*, Web. 2006. www.tienve.org/home/literature/viewLiterature.do;jsessionid=E3A-3D434A3E44324BDF6BA32FBE7AC29?action=viewArtwork&artworkId=4415

Trần Ngọc Hiếu. "Cuộc nổi loạn của ngôn từ trong thơ đương đại, ghi nhận qua một số hiện tượng." ["The Rebellion of the Word in Contemporary Poetry, Perceived through Several Phenomena."] *Talawas*, Web. 12 May 2005. www.talawas.org/talaDB/showFile.php?res=4476&rb=06

—."Góp phần nhận diện thơ trẻ những năm đầu thế kỉ." ["A Contribution to Identifying Young Poets in the New Millennium."] *Talawas*, Web. August 2005.

—."Nhà thơ – bạn đọc trong đời sống văn học hôm nay." ["The Poet and the Reader in Literary Life Today."] *Talawas*, Web. November 2005.

—. (An Vân) "Góp thêm lời bàn về một dòng thơ mới." ["Additional Commentaries on a New Poetry Genre."] *Talawas*, Web. 5 April 2006. www.talawas.org/talaDB/showFile.php?res=6861&rb=0205

—."Viết thơ là gì – Tiếp cận một số thực hành thơ ca hiện nay từ hành động viết." ["How to Define Poetry-Writing: On Contemporary Poetic Practices as Acts of Writing."] *Contemporary Vietnamese Poetry Conference*. Hồ Chí Minh: Hồ Chí Minh City University of Social Sciences and Humanities Press, 2008. Print.

—."Trò chơi như một khuynh hướng trong thơ Việt Nam đương đại." ["Play as a Disposition in Vietnamese Contemporary Poetry."] *Những cạnh khía của lịch sử văn học* [Edges of Literary History]. Edited by Đỗ, Lai T., Hà Nội: Writers' Association Press, 2016. Print.

Trúc Linh. "Nhóm Mở Miệng với thứ rác rưởi được gọi là thơ." ("The Open Mouth Group with Trash Called Poetry.") *City Police*, December 22, 2005.

The Possibilities and Limits of Play: Poetry and [Self-]publishing Practices in Việt Nam Today
written in English by Nhã Thuyên

Straining to give poetic existences visibility through acts of writing and publishing that I have undertaken without knowing where they will lead me, I prefer to envision the effort as an inspirational encounter rather than an ambitious idea, as a dream of community rather than a promised vision, as a poetic means rather than a pragmatic goal. In this essay, through exposing some fragments of the generally outdated quixotic adventure stories bound up in passions for literature, I want to question the possibilities and I within the limitations of poetry's connection to practices of independent [self-]publishing, which continues to bear the label of "underground" or "unofficial" publishing in Việt Nam today and thus cannot be detached from attempts to understand censorship and freedoms of expression. On a personal note, I waded through writing and rewriting the three parts of this essay many times, spanning over five years and evolving into these fragments as the most possible form, a form not detached from my own experience as an intuitive observer, a maker, and a writer.

Fragment 1
Sidewalk Publishing: A Political and Aesthetic Venture Rallying in the Streets

I quote here—and will reiterate it elsewhere in another of my essays—a few lines from the noteworthy preamble of Nguyễn Quốc Chánh's e-book *Của căn cước ẩn dụ (Of Metaphorical Identity)*, published online with *Talawas* in late 2001; a pioneering agitation against the strenuous task of requesting I purchasing publishing permission by using the internet as a newly discovered space:

> Writing, printing, and publishing with permission is a
> method of providing a helping hand to the reactionary, as

a way of "giving them enough rope to hang themselves."

It does not give the reactionary much of a push, it only adds more accomplices to the conspiracy to smother individual freedom.

I have just a few dozens of acquaintances, a handful of friends, and only with computer civilization can my poetry be read cleanly without having to stoop or squeeze through any inspections

At nearly the same time as Nguyễn Quốc Chánh's ebook, self-publishing in print-book form was quickly blossoming into a movement as well, particularly around 2003 to 2008 in Sài Gòn, with the collectivization of several writers and artists of various ages. A series of books streamed into to life, with the excitement of collaborative improvisation among friends, thanks to a series of publishers existing on the margins: Giấy Vụn (Scrap Paper Press), Lá Chuối (Banana Leaf), Con Rùa (Turtle), Tùy Tiện (As You Like), Kông Kốc (Vain Labor), Cửa (Door), Da Vàng (Yellow Skin), Điếu Cày (Bamboo Pipe), Lề Bên Trái (Left Margin), Tân Hình Thức (New Formalism), Minh Châu (the publisher's name), and so on. From this scene, enduring for the past 15 years, and with persistently expanding notions of publishing, Giấy Vụn, the press behind the Mở Miệng poetry group, leaves a truly remarkable and lasting imprint. And while their publications of poetry may have gradually quieted down, in recent years Giấy Vụn and other unlicensed publishers can be seen producing works on the literary fringes, filling in the gaps of the official publishing sphere, including Vietnamese translations of such works as *Animal Farm* and *1984* by George Orwell, *The Power of the Powerless* by Václav Havel, and many others.

To engage in self-publishing, more popularly called photocopy I samizdat I illegal I fringe I underground I informal I independent I alternative publishing, or in Việt Nam where the sidewalk is a spontaneous public space for writers and artists, the most common term—sidewalk publishing—has become a highly conscious choice of writers who do not wish to bend their pens. Trần Tiến Dũng stated, when self-publishing by photocopy his third collection of poetry, entitled *Mây bay là bay rồi (Floating Clouds Have Already Floated Away)*:

> I am not surprised that the regime and exclusive publishing system lost their civilized behavior in "buying" the dream of beautiful and untainted poetry. [...] Poetry gives me love and my love for poetry fills me with a craving for freedom and human rights.
>
> —Trần Tiến Dũng

Appearing to be an alternative and confrontational stance against the strict system of external censorship, the choice to self-publish emerges from the need for self-expression, as well as from a people's right to argue the legitimacy of official laws and propose their necessary expansion. It can be an assembly to test restrictions, or to test the breakability of such restrictions in order to create a more open assembly.

I would love to mention here the e-book and print-on-demand systems as other means of self-publishing. *Da Màu* magazine first initiated and built an independent Vietnamese ebook system, providing free access to readers inside the country, with the great hopes for an "E-book Revolution" which would ensure a book's intact existence, keeping it free from the government interventions that might ban it or remove it from circulation, as well as reducing the pressures of printing costs and taking advantage of unlimited editions and global distribution (Phùng Nguyễn). Online magazines based overseas, such as the Berlin-based *Talawas* (now deactivated), Sydney-based *Tiền Vệ* and the U.S-based *Da Màu*, as well as blogs, forums, and other social networks, have also become spaces for the self-publishing of poetry. In recent years, a greater difficulty for domestic book-printing due to economic and security reasons has impelled some authors and independent publishers, such as Giấy Vụn to adopt print-on-demand methods, in which books are digitally printed only in response to customer orders. However, the potential and impact online spaces have had on experimental poetry and publishing practices needs another examination. Compared to these sidewalk publications, online publishing seems to have functioned more as a means of self-regulated media, taking a supporting role to promote one's printed books rather than a main role in exploring language and poetic experimentation. Printed books and their hand-to-hand distribution networks on the other hand seem to offer more inspiration, with more adventurous practices piquing the curiosity of more readers and thus the increasing concern of the authorities.

A Playground of Poetic Experiments:
Giấy Vụn as a Case Study

How has the practice of independent publishing created a playground of poetic experiments without conceding to the multi-layered web of a state censorship system? Those Vietnamese poets who publish independently have not hesitated to violate and break taboos; they have nakedly exposed themselves and readily used their biographies and their bodies as poetic materials. Themes of politics and sex quite clearly burst forth as poetic forms. Both intentional and unintentional disregard for standardization has occurred at various levels, from the design of book covers, layouts, and types of paper, to the content itself, from an earlier period of hastily bound limited edition photocopies with lighthearted | heavyhearted visual poems, to later books including a press logo and using the offset print method, requiring a minimum of 500 copies for each run. The publishers too have operated using alternative methods: without the need to | care for selling books, they have been more concerned with how to keep their books out of the sight and reach of cultural security guards, and how to give | distribute | disperse their books safely to readers' hands. The products (the books) have seemed less important than the very process of making them: an experiment and experience of free expression, of eagerness, of surprises in toddling, of tottering, incautious, insecure, with looming risk, and sometimes discouragement. The presence of such books indeed witnesses the presence of a concept on publishing that is gradually taking shape, with or without a clear articulation: to publish poetry is to experiment and attempt to build a readership. The most poetical aspect of these publishing practices, to me, lies in their [anti-]aesthetic venture, or their aesthetic venture that runs counter to official practices in Việt Nam of the past few decades.

Among sidewalk publishers, Giấy Vụn distinguishes itself through a number of collective and personal projects and anthologies of poetry. A few noteworthy projects include the collection of Trash poetry, Filthy poetry, and Cemetery poetry called *có jì ∂ùng jì, có nấy ∂ùng nấy (got ∂is use ∂is, got ∂at use ∂at)* with poetry collections of Mở Miệng's group members (Lý Đợi, Bùi Chát, Khúc Duy); various anthologies of domes-tic- or foreign-based writers such as *Vòng tròn sáu mặt (Six-Sided Circle)*, *Mở Miệng, 13 tác giả (13 Authors)*, *Khoan cắt bê tông (Cutting and Drilling Concrete)*, 47; a series of "old stories, new narratives" that "recover the past" with titles parodying those of well-known Vietnamese medieval heritage, such as *Lĩnh Đinh chích khoái (A Selection of Linh Dinh's Pleasures)* imitating the title *Lĩnh Nam chích quái (Mysterious Tales from Linh Nam Province)*, which is thus far Linh Dinh's only collection of poetry in Viet-namese, or works keeping their original titles such as *Lĩnh Nam tạp lục (Reciting a Variety of Stories from Linh Nam)* by Vương Văn Quang, or *Luận ngữ tân thư (The Analects of Confucius' New Book)* by Phạm Lưu Vũ. To introduce Giấy Vụn's early editions, I quote from the commentary of Vietnamese diaspora poet Nguyễn Đăng Thường, in an interview series conducted by Trần Tiến Dũng:

> The cover of the poetry collection *thơ jác từ jười (jubbish poetry from jefuse)* is brown. The front cover is entirely blank, as an abstract painting. The back cover is a figure of a half-naked female beauty, wearing long black stockings up to the groin, an artwork by Egon Schiele, an Austrian artist living in Vienna in early 20th century, who belongs to "decadent" group of artists (Klimt, Kokoschka, and others), those whose art was burned during Hitler's regime. At the bottom of the back cover, a sentence by Tadeusz Rózewics: "I can't understand that poetry should survive when

the men who created that poetry were dead. One of the premises and incentives for my poetry is a disgust with poetry. What I revolted against was that it had survived the end of the world, as though nothing had happened." The quote is taken from the pages of "Central-European Poetry" translated into Vietnamese by Thường Quán, though [Giấy Vụn] mistakenly recorded the source as *"Tạp Chí Thơ (Poetry Magazine) issue 19, spring 2000"* instead of autumn (correct). Generally speaking, I see it quite successful in terms of its aesthetics. Its content, its platform, its subversion has been loudly demolished with applause already, so I will leave these aside. However, if there must be a polite response to the building criticism, I could add: Dada has not yet died, it is still today robust and globally present. As Mark Twain, William Faulkner, and other authors spoke of the poor whites and Southern black slaves, so too the Open Mouth group speaks. Filthy poetry doesn't create more rubbish. Filthy poetry only takes rubbish from the regime and throws it back. Ordinary life here is the disordered day in the life on alley 47, is a lame cunt of a mediocre cock.

    —Nguyễn Đăng Thường

The book covers warn of danger for "those poetry readers who are faint of heart" (Giấy Vụn's words) and bring desacralized laughter to a visual surface. I should note that book covers and book design are always strictly controlled in official publishing houses in Việt Nam, with any "strange" or "challenging" marker potentially leading cultural authorities to criticize or remove the book from circulation for reasons such as "violating good habits and fine customs."

Some sidewalk publishing books:

Image 7.1 Cailonboɗi (Thecuntleft) by Bùi Chát (2004).

Nhã Thuyên

Image 7.2 Front cover Xin lỗi chịu hổng nổi (Sorry Can't Stand It) by Bùi Chát (2007).

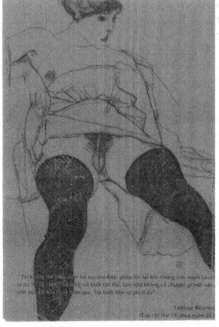

Image 7.3 Back cover: Xaùo choän chong ngaøy (Däily ùpheavals) by Bùi Chát (December, 2003).

Image 7.4 Front cover: Khoan cắt bê tông (Drilling and Cutting Concrete), a collection of 23 authors (2005). The cover displays the popular words posted on city walls: "No climbing" "Deadly danger".

Image 7.5 Front cover: Ê, tao đây (Hey, I'm Here) by Nguyễn Quốc Chánh (2004).

Image 8: A set of books published by various sidewalk presses. Image courtesy of © AI.

Samizdat and More

I quote here from the famous lines of poet Vladimir Bukovsky: "Samizdat: I write it myself, edit it myself, censor it myself, publish it myself, distribute it myself, and spend jail time for it myself." One feature of the publishing conditions in Việt Nam today is the popular and recently legalized [semi-]cooperation between state-run publishing houses and private ones. In fact, many state-run publishing houses survive solely by selling licenses to private publishers, and such private companies can only lean in the direction of legally independent publishing through their economic cooperation with the state. However, the market and pressurized control of "sensitive elements" still weigh heavily on writers, mentally and practically.

A featured series of essays on samizdat in *Poetics Today*, Winter 2008 issue offer several references and suggestions for understanding and approaching these phenomena.

Such conditions situate the sidewalk publishing of Việt Nam today as a locally contextualized response that can refer back to past *samizdat* practices of Eastern Europe and the post-Stalin Soviet Union, while at the same time, these practices are not separate from contemporary trends of alternative publishing, using the advantages of design and printing technology as well as the convenience of production and the distribution capabilities of the internet. The concern here is ambiguity and the lack of a legalized framework to ensure independent publishing; although these sidewalk publications are not absolutely prohibited by law, the practices are nonetheless punishable, with publishers and distributors facing the risk of jail.

However, I think it would be superficial and unjustified to differentiate between radical and conservative literature simply by its method of publication. Just as it would be a cruel and harsh repression for official Vietnamese media to continue labeling these sidewalk publications as "poisonous products," or to explain the existence of alternative publishing merely as dissident action. The authors themselves hold different perspectives and approaches: some may consider official publishing synonymous with an acceptance of the state censorship system which violates their own professional ethics, while others can more or less flexibly navigate these spaces. What I wish to emphasize here is how the poets who do not accept external systems of censorship, who are not involved in any state-run institutions or groups, who are being marginalized or marginalizing themselves, who choose to publish independently or underground, all share an idea of being independent individuals with the desire to represent themselves in their literary works. Surely no one wants to be [self-]excluded from literary conversations and to [self-]limit their readership.

I have come to think that to interpret the nature of alternative publishing solely within the so-called contemporary local political context is too narrow an explanation. Its intersection with another tradition of poetry (perhaps a particularly eastern one) is often unconsidered: that of composing, sharing, and enjoying poetry as the intimate essence of "being oneself." In this traditional sense, poetry was *naturally* self-published: as a specific communication between kindred literary spirits, poetry was engraved and printed, or handwritten in single edition, to keep as one's own possession or to send to a confidant. Poetry most concerns its readers, especially the intimate soul-sharing ones. One famous allusion from the East: Bo Ya breaks his seven-stringed zither when Zhong Ziqui passes away. And without his soulmate, the Vietnamese Nguyễn Khuyến (1835-1909), laments: "Viết đưa ai, ai biết mà đưa?"/ "Write for whom, who could know?" With print technology, poetry gradually becomes a modern profession; poetry publishing then is concerned with the market and poets themselves concerned with selling poetry: "Văn chương hạ giới rẻ như bèo / Literature on earth is cheap as dirt" (Tản Đà, 1889-1939). And another concern added to the list, as in Việt Nam today: that which is "unprintable" for political censorship. The fact is that the permission to publish poetry in Việt Nam, as it is provided by the state, often exposes some contradictions: on the one hand, it is extremely easy to obtain or purchase permission to publish poetry, on the other hand, the names of poets are rigorously scrutinized, whether or not the content of their work contains "sensitive" material. The same goes for poetry's circulation: the simple act of reciting, passing along, handwriting a poem one loves, even simply playing with a few lines, can become an issue of biblical proportion. Often an unexpected gift follows the poetry: a stalker, an interrogation, the removal of lines, the loss of employment, the isolation and exclusion from literary activities, a ban, and not so rarely, a trial. Vietnamese writers living within the country today do not easily forget that the demands to "be oneself" when writing and publishing poetry can lead to terrible consequences.

Recalling my poetry collection *Rìa vực* (*The Edge of the Abyss*), published by Giấy Vụn in 2011, I want to consider my participation with sidewalk publishing from the perspective of an author who became involved by way of an opportunity rather than a principled intention, to modestly practice the ideal of not dividing literature by methods of literary production. My poetry—often considered apolitical—did not have difficulty getting official permission, and, therefore, as some friends advised me, it was not necessary to publish with a sidewalk publisher. In 2010, the legally independent publishing house that had released my debut collection in 2007, a house run almost entirely by just one person who was filled with a passion for poetry and great caring for young writers, fell into financial difficulty more than halfway through the process of giving birth to my book. My book, among other titles, was eventually abandoned and the publishing company closed down not long after. I then revised the manuscript and sent it out to my friends at Giấy Vụn. Experimenting with the underground publishing model, with xerox printing (the book was even mistakenly cut into two different sizes, 12x21cm and 13x21cm), with books not sold but rather donated as gifts to friends, I experienced poetry being cared for in and as friendship; the means of publishing, whether officially or unofficially, whether with a big or small publisher, became less important than the way poetry was born, how it emerged and reached its readers. As an aside, I would like to mention that all sidewalk publications, excluding those copies in the hands of the cultural police, are kept safe and disseminated by a network of writers and poets, a few close readers, some book collectors and book lovers here and there, who accept their role of involvement.

I continue to believe that this community of writers and readers involved in sidewalk publishing and independent presses has played an important role in Việt Nam, as the keepers of such fragile experiments and existences of poetry as well and the unique lives of poets. Another extended aside I would like to add here: I am always reluctant to talk about the professionalism of writing and publishing poetry in Việt Nam. Though there may be "a poet on every corner," to be a poet here is mostly an embarrassing label and by no means a "profession" or, to many, it is a degenerate job for those who do not know how to better use their lives. National literary awards or funding from the state are seemingly unfamiliar to most Vietnamese writers, while the few privatized awards for published poetry have since ceased after their initiation. The qualities of self-publishing are clearly evident even in the official sector: often a book of poetry exists outside the so-called publishing market because, with the exception of those "books of | for the state," most poets reach into their own pockets to buy permission and print their poetry, which is then predominantly self-distributed to friends and others around the poetry circles. It is for this that poetry copyright laws are of little concern, exemplified by the popular play of words in which a copyright signifies the "right to copy," or intentionally generous giving. The expectation of poetic exchanges is more or less met by the choice to work within sidewalk publishing: poets can embrace the joy of sharing and being shared among a more or less familiar and distinguished community of friends removed from the mainstream. Of course, there are some concerns with such methods of publishing: a diminished community consisting only of those who already know each other, and the fact that these books have never (yet) appeared in library archives or on the shelves of state-run bookstores, nor have they ever been reviewed or mentioned in official newspapers.

Originating as a collective response to a system of state censorship, one can see that sidewalk publishing has gradually grown into a strategy of survival and presence. This strategy works to neutralize the privileged power of the state-run publishing system while connecting literary individuals. It creates some conditions to combat the isolation of writers and accompany the exploration of aesthetics and experimentation with alternative methods, which are born out of the desire to protect the life of poetic voices under political and economic pressure. To me, the most positive aspect of these literary publications, running parallel to other kinds of experimental and independent art, is the significant contribution they make to the enduring processes of self-definition and self-representation among marginalized groups and individuals, as well as alternative spaces. It would be a regrettable oversight to approach contemporary Vietnamese art and literature without recognizing the existence of this unofficial sphere, with the peripheries excluded from official cultural life, as they contain an interesting array of literary materials, if not the most vivid and moving.

Fragment 2
AJAR: A Possibility of Play

I imagine a playground where Vietnamese poetry is present without the haunting chains of an external censorship system. A place where Vietnamese poetry can be read and collide with other languages. Where drifting adventures meet, often unexpectedly, and share experi(ence)ments, aesthetic questions, generously and fruitfully. Where the writing of poetry is not detached from the reading of poetry, and the distribution of poetry in its community is not merely the distribution of manufactured products but rather a distribution of sense and beauty. Ideas of sharing in language through publishing started to take concrete shape in late 2013 when Kaitlin Rees and I, though certainly inexperienced, began to sketch a website, to read and translate poetry together, and make some very first books to nurture a toddling AJAR with the companionship of friends.

AJAR is something unprecedented in Hà Nội: self-funded and unaffiliated with either outside organizations or national institutions, the press is run by writers and sustained by their personal resources, as well as the support of readers. As self-introduced on the website:

> AJAR is dedicated to the discovery of poetry and art in both ordinary and hidden places, providing a space for these works to be exhibited, loved, and challenged. As a bilingual journal and independent small press based in Hà Nội, AJAR provides an opening for questions, imaginings, and poetic (im)possibility to be shared across borders, inhabiting language as it moves between worlds and words. In bringing fresh and critical voices of Vietnamese literature and art into English, and welcoming those voices from everywhere into Vietnamese, we focus on quality translations and envision books as artifacts of artistic collaboration.

In terms of intention, AJAR operates not as a mode of independent publishing with aims of confronting censorship in Việt Nam. As such, we do not simply promote self-publishing acts and banned works for political reasons, nor do we desire to be a deviant thorn in the system. Rather, AJAR works to create a coexisting space, to preserve love for the solitary voice, to be occupied with exploration, to welcome the possibilities of writing and reading, to embrace the admirers, to invite poetic exchanges in a supportive community of friendship and love. The language of resistance is foreign to our way of thinking, though battle itself may be a constant; in being reluctant to follow the well-worn paths, I can never finish questioning the limits and possibilities of attempts at coexistence.

Lacking legal security, the total absence of support from official media outlets limits distribution of the poetry products: without the right to sell at state-run bookstores, AJAR books are sold in independent bookstores only, which are scarce and highly controlled in Việt Nam, or they are passed from hand to hand through networks of friends, exhibited in a few cafes and galleries, or sold through an online shop. Distribution is more focused on an enduring sensibility: to make books and hand them over to readers as beautiful artifacts that give a presence to Vietnamese poetry, Vietnamese poetry in translation, and translations from other languages into Vietnamese. Reading new works or new authors gives us a chance to destabilize an aesthetic establishment and open ourselves up to perceive others. Possibilities of conversation between readers and writers spring from the pages of books, from the website, and from related events. Languages expand us: each issue of AJAR's journal opens one word to explore in meaning and signification, as an open dictionary. The act of choosing a work to translate and publish is sometimes quite personal: we meet works that we'd love to see reborn in another language; we meet and become fond of authors and their languages; writers seek each other, a certain writer seeks us. There are those who have achieved fame, there are those just starting out. There are those who come and return, there are those who come and leave. There is care taken to balance the works from Vietnamese language with those from other languages—not only English, as the familiar faces with the absent or remote presences.

The question of [self-]representation in translation parallels the need to exchange. To self-publish is to represent oneself and one's friends and associates. To translate poetry is to enact the original inside another language. The self-representation occurs when the work of translation emerges from the very need of self-expanding the original language, to not be isolated and monotonous in its own world, and from here a conversation may initiate, on how we could be read in others' languages and how we could invite others in. I have not considered being translated and represented in English as something "international," but as an appreciation for the relationships between writing and reading found in another language. Expansion of the self lies in its encounters, not a reinforcement of any privilege: I, as a human, always need to converse, and in a more or less intimate space, if my dear friends are speaking a language that is not my mother tongue, I would love to utter my own tongue to converse with them. Falling into these languages, I learn how to be with them: an insecure love with a language I thought I knew, an anxious love with a language to which I am a stranger, all are adventures, educations, attempts to understand the languages of the loved ones.

I hold stubbornly to the belief that there are neither major nor minor languages; the distance between languages connects living curiosities. Each language possibly carries its own (dis)ability for its nước.country.water.poetry, and perhaps poetry has its own people who care for its languages. Translators, like the ones circulating around AJAR, for the most part work out of love for an author or their fondness for probing into languages. Why do I want to introduce Vietnamese poetry into English, and vice versa, and who will care about it? I feel a hesitance around "aboutness" when it comes to the significant work of presenting poetry into other languages, particularly introducing yet-to-be-known literature into more widely read languages. To me, first and foremost, poetry continues to be where the unlimited specificity of cultural differences can be held and tolerated, where the otherness of languages can be embraced, and the act of translating, therefore, can create chances to encounter different ways of thinking and feeling, to enlarge a better understanding of myself and others.

At its core, I hope for AJAR to be as a transformation, for its more or less joyful community to keep expecting encounters with a real presence—equal and inspirational—rather than with more industrial products that try to enter the market; I work toward for the continued efforts of nurturing and expanding languages rather than blindly promoting any singular/single-path of ideology.

Image 8: AJAR books. Image courtesy © AJAR 2017.

Fragment 3
Writing: (Not Even) A Choice

Perhaps there are no more than two choices: to write or not write. Perhaps this is the choicelessness of writing: to choose "write" means to be responsible for the [personal] freedom of [self-]expression, to choose to remain uncensored by any external body. I write this not to deny the fact that we, particularly those of us in red-listed countries where freedom of expression appears to be a "necessary luxury," must still strive to "have" or "reach a certain level" of freedom by demanding concrete rights that can be bullet-pointed, labeled, and guaranteed by some recognized system or institution; and of course we must not cease discussing, rethinking, reshaping, re-understanding freedom

EN: One is reminded of Audre Lorde's essay, "Poetry Is Not A Luxury" which argues, "poetry is not a luxury. It is a vital necessity of our existence. It forms the quality of the light within which we predicate our hopes and dreams toward survival and change, first made into language, then into idea, then into more tangible action."

of expression, its status, its vision, even its hopeless dream. I write this not to delude myself in an abstract feeling of freedom in front of the white page of my computer, but to converse on it, as practicing the possibilities of freedom of expression and of self-control | self-censorship that I think no one can easily deprive a writer.

Hence, as a writer, I often do not truly understand the way someone can speak about censorship as something outside of oneself, or as if censorship does not exist here but it exists there, that there is more censorship here and less of it there, that writers here only need to face themselves while writers there are always accompanied by some horrific monsters with scary and powerful scissors, or that writers here are happier | suffering more for their writing and playful experiments, while writers there are happier | suffering more for having something to fight for. Therefore, one direction of thinking and acting that I personally want to avoid is the way some writers try to make use of and benefit off of censorship when it comes to the competitive relations to powers. Occasionally it can be useful: writers and artists can use the monstrous figures to parody, to exploit as a theme, to create strategic metaphors around, taking advantage of the situation to win exposure, to win attention in order to introduce great works and authors, to raise their voices; and at very least, in some moments, some curious crowds might stop to listen, and there might occur some lucky chances of exchange and discussion. Winning attention through censorship and taking advantage of censorship to get more attention is a situation not unfamiliar to writers and artists in certain countries, such as Việt Nam. But I would love to push further, to ask: who is paying attention to whom, and why is this one paying attention to us more impressive and somehow more valuable than that one? The distinctions between positions of me and you, us and the other, this other and that other, are perhaps the subtle and personal relations between all of humanity, but it raises doubt if these distinctions lead to power relations in which this one wants to control and monitor the other one.

Another aspect, regarding the ease of going between the scissors, in the narrow space where one accepts to be controlled, or the passivity and even comfort of accepting the seemingly unchangeable status quo, may reveal a blind spot in public discourse. I do not think that Vietnamese writers and artists today can still feel satisfied with "the rule" that they can "speak freely about everything, as long as it does not touch politics." This meager freedom of expression offered as propaganda, circumscribed inside the fear of being imprisoned, interrogated, or banned, led to the beautifully brave reactions of those who refused to compromise, who would not be accomplice to official powers—which meant their marginalization and other risks. Of course, no one would want to exchange getting attention for the risk of being imprisoned, or interrogated, or maligned in the *People's Newspaper* or State Television. Such actions and reactions, as with the unexpected and terrible consequences that result, can thus be seen as a practice of following personal truths, of living in the possibility of freedom, and are undertaken with diverse understanding and strategies. The courage and dreams of certain pioneering writers who are determined to commit their own lives to an intentional freedom, while aware of its limits, have invited bolder attitudes, more eager minds, and moved more young hearts, even perhaps only inch by inch, to be more enduring in their love of literature.

However, I would love to push the story of censorship to its edges, to discuss a kind of censorship not visible in handcuffs, prisons, bans, withdrawals, or deprivation, but rather an inner, complex, and delicate self-censorship I self-control: that of the comfortable within literature and art. The intention to be comforting, whether it be to state criteria, to publishing systems, to markets, comforting to this or that other, can be seen as a practice of subtle censorship, one that can even be praised. The complicity, sometimes in the appearance of agreements or congeniality between writers and readers, creators and enjoyers, is where literature has to face perhaps a more unfortunate truth: we, as writers and readers, have not ceased building more frames for creation and enjoyment and interpretation, frames to monitor taste and classify readers as highbrow or common, to make a hierarchy of values and oppress the existence of this one while praising another, and ignoring or avoiding confrontation with some issues of life and art. In a noisy public space, the personal voices, often vulnerable, know they cannot become fighters simply to comfort or satisfy others. So how to survive, to survive beautifully without being harmed and silenced? How to accompany writers and readers inside the scissors of the practical world? I've known not just a few of my fellow writers and friends who have somehow decided to quit writing, or at least, who have stopped appearing in public and in print, along with several pioneering Vietnamese writers who have now become totally silent. There are those of them who believe they are failures, defeated on the path of loving literature. But perhaps what they feel is the hopelessness of not ever being shared in a community, the fear of not being understood, of not having any intimate soul-sharing readers, of soliloquizing, with perhaps at some point the protracted suffering of a violently oppressed inner world. Perhaps it is this that reaches into the darkest depths of a writer and suddenly cuts them in half.

This is where I want to rethink censorship and freedom of expression. I envision how freedom of expression could open a seemingly not-for-profit conversation: I experiment with my speech and writing, and expect to be listened to, to be explored, to be a contribution. To treasure the personal attempts of those who do not easily accept what is comfortable, including not only writers but also readers, to limit the harmful judges of each individual, and to add no more poison into public spaces. Aimlessness and playfulness are attached to the need for understanding, and more, they create a playground for understanding, for the equal existences of I, you, he, she, it, they, and all of us. Inside this space I [plural] cannot avoid facing the personal questions: to what extent do I want my freedom, how to gradually reduce the fear that keeps me from voicing my experiments, how to be ceaselessly vigilant about the risks of accepting self-censorship and comforting solutions.

And so, I no longer think along the lines of "demanding the right to speak." With resistance itself often raising ethical dilemmas, a writer can be easily misunderstood in some societies if making the choice to not directly confront power systems and instigate battles as a dissident. The choice of following a writing | living practice that is not concerned with offering comforts, that even makes it difficult to feel comforted, can be a risky one: most of the time, it has the look of play, of lacking responsibility or participation, of stepping away from life; it has the look of escapist dreamers in their "ivory tower of art;" it has the sad and deserted look of loners, of strangers, of outsiders, of those to whom it is not easy to speak, of those whose companions are still absent. The choice to be a writer, one who refuses complicity, who occasionally expects to be heard, among millions of voices, who demands more patience and endurance, to be a writer who perhaps simply bears witness to their own aesthetics and ethics for the whole of their writing life, such choices can often feel intense and hopeless.

I don't think the story of my case is exceptional in Việt Nam, a country where writers and artists, even those living a mostly pure life with words, cannot seem to maintain their ability to be surprised by the absurd turbulence storming down on their works. I still struggle with how to tell my own story—one I feel a responsibility to tell as it is not simply a personal story I should hold onto myself. The case, publicized on state media, reviews my position and my "morality" as a lecturer at the Hà Nội National University of Education, after concerns were raised regarding my project of underground voices in the Vietnamese poetry scene during the post-Renovation period. The project was published on the US-based *Da Màu* magazine, and my Master's degree thesis, titled "Positioning the periphery: poetry practices of the Mở Miệng group as a cultural phenomenon," was submitted in 2011 to the Hà Nội National University of Education, where I would later become a lecturer. I lost my job and my professor was fired after numerous articles were published by official media condemning the author—and later the professor—as "reactionary," "poisonous," "political dissidents" who "attack the Party", etc.

with unbelievably biting judgments. It was a highly successful oppression using blatant intimidation of academics and individuals: despite there being several petitions and articles from writers and scholars to protect me, the thesis, and the Master's certification were still revoked. From the first slandering article in May 2013, to official condemnation of the thesis in March 2014, until now in 2017, my works and communication in the field of literature continue to be impeded or restricted in some way. In a recent interview conducted by Vietnamese diaspora writer Phùng Nguyễn, I was asked if I thought my silence or reticence was an instance of me being too passive and indifferent to my victim status in this case, and if I ever regretted that behavior.

As I personally do not choose a path of direct resistance to power systems, instead rejecting the dualism of resistance and oppression, I deny the label(ing) of a "dissident writer." I do not think that this choice is at all synonymous with passivity or silence or a refusal to fight. I admit that I am one victim of an oppressive system, between issues of academic freedom and freedom of speech, but I am also aware that I choose to follow and rely on the possibilities of being a single human, often casting doubt on established standards, and reducing in myself the ambition to bear any message besides that of being. To the interviewer I answered: "I am interested in questions of social justice not being separate from the concerns for an individual's equality. Hence, the intention and choice to protect, rely on, and pursue my personal value of equality and justice perhaps does not fit inside the common profile for justice that another or several others may have" (Phùng Nguyễn). I suppose my personal ideas and actions are of little use to the people whose expectations I do not match, particularly to those who supported and protected me as a victim with the simple need to reclaim justice.

In refusing to reduce myself to a victim status, I refuse the anticipated behaviors of a victim. I want to respond to the voices by the act of writing, by provoking myself to keep writing. To experiment with and experience independent publishing

116

modes in Việt Nam can be seen as an invitation to dialogue, to share, to argue, to be critical, consistently, and sometimes with exhaustion, doubt, and desperation, but trying to be patient.

Ultimately, to practice freedom of expression, for me, is to practice observing, contemplating, and experiencing a kind of personal truth, on the written page, a truth not easily censored. Not self-censoring who I am and who I am becoming affords me the opportunity to listen, watch, admire, touch, sense, and better understand. I still believe no mode of society naturally offers complete freedom. I [plural] choose to write or not write. I [plural] choose to be expanded or to be self-limited. The word *censorship* remains in use; it reminds us not of our fear but of its needless abundance. And so, while not hiding my support and respect for critical movements in society and literature, I am more engaged in attempts for poetic conversation, as a means to heal the fragmented beings and in some way, to be healed myself. Perhaps the story of Việt Nam must be told by the Vietnamese people, as the stories of other countries must be told by their citizens, to erase the fear of an inability to speak for oneself, but the stories of Việt Nam and elsewhere could also be told by anyone, as an attempt to erase the power inherent in the ability to speak out, and the privileges of speaking out.

In the end, it is impossible for writers to cease experimenting and performing their abilities of speech, waiting for that speech to be shared, accepting the numerous consequences of it. And there is nothing besides the written page, which we face alone, surrounded by demons, and all the ways of writing and living, to which perhaps each writer must spend their whole life bearing witness.

Work Cited

Nguyễn Đăng Thường, Trần Tiến Dũng. "Chung quanh sự kiện các tác phẩm văn chương xuất bản dưới hình thức photocopy ở Sài Gòn." ["On Literary Works Published in Photocopied Mode in Sài Gòn."] *Tiền Vệ*, Web. http://www.tienve.org/home/music/viewMusic. do;jsessionid=36A326E1DC739446A8E5FCDF929F-%209C15?action=viewArtwork&artworkId=4491

Nguyễn Quốc Chánh. *Của căn cước ẩn dụ*. [Of Metaphorical Identity.] Translation by David Payne. Ebook, *Talawas*, 2001.

Nhã Thuyên. *Mở Miệng: Cuộc nổi dậy của rác thải [Open Mouth: The Revolt of Rubbish.]* Translation by Quyên Nguyễn, manuscript.

Phùng Nguyễn. "Cuộc cách mạng ebook." ["Ebook Revolution."] *Da Màu*, Web. April 2011. http://damau.org/archives/19535.

—."Ba câu hỏi cho Nhã Thuyên." ["Three Questions for Nhã Thuyên."] *Vietnamese VOA Radio*, August, 2015. Web. www.voatiengviet.com/content/ba-cau-hoi-cho-nha- thuyen/2933651.html

Trần Tiến Dũng. "Mây bay là bay rồi." ["Floating Clouds Have Already Floated Away."] *Sài Gòn: Photocopied Poetry*, 2010. Web. *Tiền Vệ*. http://tienve.org/home/images/trantiendung-maybaylabayroi.pdf

Poetry of Negation and the Negation of Poetry
translated by Ngân Nguyễn

In the wake of the ill-fated narratives between poetry and politics in Việt Nam, my concern in this essay is with the emergence in recent decades of a genre normally bracketed as dissident poetry. There seems to be a pervasive message that poets should bear in mind poetry's obligation to be socially engaged and that the most engaged genre of all is political poetry, purporting to raise awareness, to fight for freedom of expression, to do battle with verses sedated by conservative ideological conditioning, and to differentiate itself from apolitical writing. How does the emergence of this genre, rarely seen in the state-run media, contribute to the literary scene or is it only worthy of interest as a social indicator? Is the label "dissident" still necessary to understand poetry and its politics, or it is just a worn-out concept? My observations and discussion in this essay will, at most, only offer up questions to which no satisfying answers can be guaranteed. On a side note, I will not discuss here the longstanding tradition of versifying by politicians whose writing and publishing of poetry seems quite removed from the joy of reading.

Post-War Disillusionment & Self-Negation

In Vietnamese literature, post-war dissenting opinions against the regime originated with poets inside the system, those who had been "Uncle Ho's soldiers," rather than from "antagonistic elements" launching attacks against the Party from the outside as is frequently charged. Post-war poetry was imbued with disillusionment: disappointment with the values of socialist realist poetry, torturous repentance over the dark side of war and the agonizing fate of the people, distress over the situation of the country, and the imperative of speaking the truth as an irrefutable manifestation of self-awareness on the part of those who write poetry and of the poetry itself. In this period, one can observe an attempt to escape the reign of Revolutionary Poetry that had dominated Northern Việt Nam for the previous thirty years (1945-1975), mainly taking the form of political romanticism I lyricism, with a laudatory tone, with themes specified according to the propaganda requirements of each period ("poetry against France," "poetry contributing to the development of a socialist society," "poetry against America," "poetry for the liberation of the South and the unification of the country," "odes to the Party, odes to Uncle Ho," and so on), and with numerous slogans serving as the lodestar for artistic creation ("literature and art are battlefronts on which the writers and artists are soldiers," literature "serves the fight, and serves the worker-peasant-soldier alliance," and "serves the struggle for unification," "poets must also do battle," and so on). Below are some lines from the renowned poem "Who? I!" written in 1987 by Chế Lan Viên and only published posthumously in the collection edited by Vũ Thị Thường, the author's wife, that can be read as an expression of painful remorse, a straightforward account of the horrifying massacre of innocent soldiers in the 1968 campaign that acknowledges an historic sin, one that he believed his exhortatory poems had abetted. I would love to note that Chế Lan Viên (1920-1989) used to refuse his past as a prominent poet from the late 1930s when participating in the August Revolution in 1945, and subsequently became a leading member of the official Writers' Association of Việt Nam—the biographical details might help to understand the position of the speaker "I" not as a personal I but a historical I, a collective I of the marching songs' writers of a time:

At Mậu Thân, 2000 people marched down to the delta
In just one night, only 30 were left
Who bears responsibility for 2000 deaths?
I!
I—the one who wrote exhortative lines
Extolling those who willingly gave their lives
in every strike.
　　　—"Who? I!", Chế Lan Viên

In the excitement following Đổi Mới (Renovation), as they were encouraged to "speak the truth," poets long affiliated with the war and with the revolutionary government seemed to have found them-selves in a new role: from veneration, professing hyperbolic affirmations of a monolatrous ideol-ogy, these poets and their poetry now mobilized to criticize society, shifting away from compliance with the policy of "poetry of and for the masses," and struggling against assimilation into a glee club of rhythmic purple prose, most notably in the case of soldier-poets such as Thanh Thảo, Nguyễn Duy, Trần Mạnh Hảo, or those of the younger generation like Đỗ Trung Quân. The headline "Things to Be Done Immediately" in the issue of *Nhân Dân* (*The People*) newspaper of 26 May 1987, written and signed by Nguyễn Văn Linh (N.V.L), the General-Secretary of the Communist Party of Việt Nam, was the first in a series of articles with a shared namesake and objective: the spirit of the Renovation Period; this series of articles inspired writers and artists to express their opinions. Initiating a dialogue with key members of the state in a similar fashion to the following poem by Thanh Thảo, that was a response to N.V.L.'s stance and pub-lished together with the article "Poetry: Courage and Unity" in *Văn nghệ* (*Arts and Letters*) Journal, they showed their ultimate faith in the system and struggled to contribute as its citizens:

> Mậu Thân (literally, the Year of the Monkey) here refers to the lunar new year (Tết) period in 1968, when the National Liberation Front (NLF) and the People's Army of North Việt Nam (PAVN) launched the Tết Offensive in Sài Gòn, Huế, and other locations throughout Southern Việt Nam.

Confession
Dear Comrade Nguyễn Văn Linh

There are times when we were extremely tired
should we call it quits, dear comrade Nguyễn Văn Linh!
you roosters in Neruda's poems

please stop crowing.
Yet crowing for the sun to rise
is in the rooster's essence.
Please do not castrate us, my dear ambitious friends,
we cannot be the plump new year offerings.
Even if the roosters do not crow
the sun will not cease to rise
you tired roosters
please step aside!
We bared our breasts at the front
we ourselves
could not go on watching any longer.
For the reformation of our fatherland
we offer again our life, our blood.

The imperative of shifting away from the assigned and directed political tone of, to take the phrase from the essay titled "Let's Give a Funeral Oration for an Era of Illustrative Literature" written in 1989 by soldier-writer Nguyễn Minh Châu, "the illustrative era of literature" (i.e. literature portraying characters and attitudes worthy of emulation, as a contribution to the war effort and to the development of a socialist society), in search of their own voice led a cohort of poets, previously utterly loyal to the official ideology, to negate their own past.

Ghosts of the Past & Dissenting Voices

The self-negating process proved insufficient, however, and it may very well be a compromise. Many of the aforementioned soldier-poets retreated to their own private corners, gradually excluding themselves from the literary scene. Another period of critical sentiment in poetry came into the equation: as the soldier-poets' desire for self-negation dwindled, dissenting voices flared up, with the aim of negating the orthodox regime and the official ideology. Poets of all ages, ranging from those born in the 50s to younger writers born in the 60s, 70s, and 80s, with varied historical experiences, residing in Việt Nam and overseas alike, were labeled "reactionary poets," e.g. Nguyễn Quốc Chánh, Trần Tiến Dũng, Phan Bá Thọ, Nguyễn Viện, the poets in the Mở Miệng group, and many others whose work has regularly been published in online literary journals based outside the country such as *Tiền Vệ* or *Da Màu*. Each of these poets has their own distinctive themes, styles, and potential impacts, but in general there has been an observable transition from constructive self-reflection to subversive criticism, and from an effort to voice the truth to an aspiration for an absolute negation, a "complete decontamination," and a nihilistic readiness to challenge and destroy.

I don't know if phrases like "democracy," "the desire for freedom," and "era," as well as numerous calls for action and expressions of discontent and frustration, might signify poetic works that are conscious of democracy and of the era in which they exist, and even enact a democratic poetics, or might simply serve to destroy their own meaning when being overused. For the most part, dissident poetry resonates against oppression, advocates for democracy, reveals previously undisclosed information, and attacks the dogma of traditional values associated with state power as well as the related opinions, authors, and works that the education system and official culture in Việt Nam have helped to glorify and to perpetuate. The desacralization of Hồ Chí Minh the icon, subversion of the persistent dominance of Hồ Chí Minh Thought, criticism of the communist system, and remarks and derisions directed against socialist realism that are present in the writings of Bùi Chát, Lý Đợi, Nguyễn Viện, Nguyễn Đăng Thường, Trần Tiến Dũng, Phan Bá Thọ, and others, come together with special features in online literary journals concerning events in the Paracel and Spratly Islands in conjunction with protests by writers, artists, and fellow democrats against communist China (especially in 2007 and 2010, in these years, protests were directed specifically at *Trung Cộng* (Communist China) rather than the more common term *Trung Quốc*–China) to constitute pervasive themes of political poetry in Việt Nam. Dissident poetry confronts the regime based on the need to destroy its monopolistic power and official ideology, linked to democratic consciousness; in a sense, this sector of poetry has become a voice of the nascent democracy movement.

I would like to borrow a poem by Bùi Chát, from his collection of political poems titled *Bài thơ một vần* (*Poem of a Single Rhyme*), to visualize the political topos of dissident poetry and its popular mode of negation. Here, the keyword "red" becomes an allegory of ideological manipulation, and thus becomes the target of the poem.

Red Light
I stand at a crossroads
Halted by the red light
People move relentlessly onward
A cool breeze at their back

We, those many generations
Held back by the red light,
We cannot lift our feet
We cannot spread our wings
Roads intersect everywhere
And no one can cross the red

We stand at a crossroads
So many generations

Only a dusty red road before us.

In the face of an intense urge to negate the status quo, of subversive intentions, of skepticism and outrage, this obsession with the color red, and the intention and need to erase it, becomes the hallmark of a generation who wish to deny their past yet can only do so with great difficulty, struggling to escape an ideology that encompasses an entire society while being fully aware of its heavy shackles.

Something significant is missing here: the politics of poetry seems to have been equated to or misunderstood as a conscious decision to embed ideology within writing, in order to comfort a concept in Việt Nam of a writer's ethical responsibility. People may discuss the paradigm shift from "following ideology down a one-way street," its direction and endpoint already flagged, to stating and taking responsibility for personal political preferences, ranging from a propagandized politics to a self-reflective politics. Yet many other questions arise. Who can decide what is ultimately correct or incorrect when it comes to the political choices of an individual, of a writer? How can one identify an ideologically-sound viewpoint, when unity has been fragmented by the ruptures, discrepancies, fractures, and collisions of the different perspectives that have become ubiquitous in Việt Nam? Can poetry have an impact as a movement for democracy, even if it sacrifices itself in a massive parade? What, at the end of the day, is truly poetry, rather than mere themes and attitudes, mere facsimiles of sporadic, disjointed individual enthusiasm? What can contribute to a transformation, to a productive divergence of poetry (its consciousness, its aesthetics) that is not just a movement or a gathering of friends and like-minded people? These are the fickle lines on which poetry perches: how can an intentionally political poem be read poetically and not just as a descriptive news article, some satirical couplets, or a pre-recorded broadcast? When is defiance a virtue and when is it merely an objective?

It seems that poetry's power of negation is not something that can be readily observed and described in slogans; even when poets present themselves as red-handed evidence of life and of oppression—choosing to defend an ideology at the cost of poetry that is also the cost of a feeble, ineffectual defense—they do not possess any power of real significance. We encounter, here and there, some moving verses; however, for the most part, the dissident poetry currently prevailing in Việt Nam evokes a disheveled, barren literary scene that matches the nihilistic ennui of individuals trying to navigate within the existing context in the country and getting stuck in ideological wars.

Historical Nihilism & the Negation of Poetry

The dominant discourses of Vietnamese history have become a topic for investigation and a target of rebellious and nihilistic attacks. I would like to mention here three poets from the South, Nguyễn Quốc Chánh, Trần Tiến Dũng (both born in 1958), and Phan Bá Thọ (born in 1972), as examples of different approaches to questioning historical narratives. The powerful blending of expressive verbal language and political representations, contemplative recapitulations of history under a teasing, provocative guise, and the distinctive individual style of each poet, all culminate in stimulating poems, to which affixing the label "dissident poetry" is perhaps unfitting. Poetry, starting from an individualistic reaction, can move towards the representation of common concerns, and poetry, by engaging with common concerns, can affirm the individual voice of its author.

Nguyễn Quốc Chánh hurls at us verses of intense negation, sweeping brush strokes that aim to erase an official history that he deems artificial, by the means of negating his own poetics. He defines himself as an individual, yet each detail in the following poem aims to represent a larger portrait of a nation and a people:

Post-, Post-, But Not Really Post- ...
From the front: my face is brazen.
From the side: my face is crooked.
From above or below: my face is foul.

Next to the Khmer: in gold I glimmer.
Next to Westerners: in confusion I deflate.
Next to the Chinese: in bashfulness I neigh.

In my last incarnation: my essence was monkey.
In this incarnation: my community are ghosts.
In my next incarnation: my nation will be a commune.

In the old days, I tattooed my body and fought the Chinese.
Now my grandpa chants jingles selling tofu.
In the past, I broke my back fending off the Westerners.
Now my dad repairs shoes on the sidewalk.
Not long ago, I sold my life fending off the Americans.
Now my wife scurries to marry a citizen of the U.S

Sometimes I want to forget: oh those who cry in solitude!
Sometimes I want to believe: oh those who cry in solitude!
Sometimes I want to go mad: oh those who cry in solitude!

The poems of Trần Tiến Dũng seem to share the same endpoint as those of Nguyễn Quốc Chánh, but they arrive by another route: deliberately uncovering an individual's internal wounds, wounds that lose their personal significance to become common concerns and, ultimately, the common concerns of the nation and its history, evolving into solutions to regenerate individual existence. In Nguyễn Quốc Chánh's poetry, there is a confrontation between the individual and the concepts of "nation" and "people" (not between the individual and the collective), while in Trần Tiến Dũng's poetry, I see various performances of the subjectivity of his fierce inner conflicts and difficult choices, processing a self-transformation through resisting his ascribed identity. Examining the progress of Trần Tiến Dũng's poetry collections in the order of their release, from the two official publications *Khối động (Moving Mass*, Trẻ Publishing House, 1997) and *Hiện (Looming into View*, Thanh Niên Publishing House, 2000), to the next three photocopied and e-book samizdat publications *Bầu trời lông gà lông vịt (Sky of Chicken and Duck Feathers*, E-Book, *Tiền Vệ*, Australia, 2003), *Hai đoá hoa trên trán cho công dân hạng hai (Two Flowers on One's Forehead for Second-rate Citizens*, Sài Gòn, 2006), and *Mây bay là bay rồi (The Floating Clouds Have Already Floated Away*, Sài Gòn, 2010), one can observe the poet's journey—from sensing his insignificance and uselessness in the search for his own individuality (outside of imposed grouping, such as the nation), to doing away with personal emotions so that he could emerge as an active participant. An attempt at erasure that is full of

Nhã Thuyên

bewilderment but seemingly inevitable. The image of a poet in a faraway land, reminiscing about his childhood fields, reminiscing over that lost habitat in the midst of the modern city, has gradually been replaced by the image of a poet roaming amongst the slings and arrows of the age, in a spontaneous and at once enduring manner, while under attack, while bearing wounds of his own volition; the tragic sentiment transcends the individual, and becomes a portrait of the common fate of the people and the community. His latest book is suffused with this resolution. I envision him amongst the long lines of people, "standing on the sidewalk and counting:"

> Again we count
> beginning from ourselves, forward and backward,
> from the sidewalk here to the crossroads there, the slaves
>   line up in
> rows
> pointing to themselves they count "one"
> pointing to their lover they count "two"...
> an invisible chain, now taut now slack, and always so very
>   long
> every time it crosses an abyss, bursting forth from the
> walls
> of cruel prisons.
> And the cold chain
> and flight after flight of sounds falling vertically into
> a squall of rain.
>   —from "We Stand on the Sidewalk and Count"

And even in a more straightforward, uncompromising, sarcastic, and yet hopeless manner, the poet defines himself: "In the Twenty-first century/me/a citizen of a communist dictatorship." ("How Nicely People Phrase It"); at the same time, he is aware that the existence and the fate of a poet cannot be separated from the context in which that poet lives|dies:

Poet! Your language enters a state of fear of the
  dictatorship to be
                                        aware of that fear
Drag out that obstinate fear and make it erupt in fear
Poet, you are not a brave man
Choose a vile pit and step out once to see if you can
  overcome it"
      —from "On Trembling Feet, I Choose to Step Out"

Trần Tiến Dũng is aware of the buried traumas and the
fractures in a poet—one who relies on language to unfold
afflictions and fears, and "to see if you can overcome it." In
those instances where he lays bare his innermost feelings, the
sensibility of a marginalized being with verses pervaded by
hopelessness, by turns obvious and subtle in his verses carry a
weight of protest that is as desperate as a lulling dose of poison:
it begins gently, and with that same gentleness people die, in
order to express their defiance.

The poetry of Phan Bá Thọ expresses protest through the
language of nihilistic derision, setting up the different kind of
play, perhaps more joyful. In his work, history has become an
"endless landfill" (Phan Bá Thọ's words) with which he can
play, and live, devoid of any restraint, pain, rage, or doubt.
Sharing the same "trash poetry" and "filthy poetry" mindset
with fellow marginalized writers Lý Đợi and Bùi Chát, in
his two samizdat volumes, *Chuyển động thẳng đứng* (*Vertical
Movement*, 2001) and *Đống rác vô tận* (*Endless Landfill*, 2004),
Phan Bá Thọ mines historical waste from news articles and old
stories, playfully converts these raw materials into poetry. The
poet revels in that rubbish heap like a scavenger:

"i am living in a vertical saigon that is starry
flashy & artificial, in fact
saigon is a wretched wench whom one can't help but love
a meaningful [& horrifying] wench"
      —from "apperceive-october"

129

Sài Gòn, once legendary, is now "a wretched wench." And in that city, Phan Bá Thọ has so often stripped himself to the skin to unflinchingly and impassively portray himself, without intention to shock anyone. One can visualize sudden seizures ambushing an electrostatic body in a unique self-portrait that could serve as an inspiration to performance artists:

a little girl with 70 years of experience rambling through
  dark alleys
an old guy—a daring rotten-manything & a rotten drunk
they, they know 80% of who i am
I'm not thuy hang or thuy hanh or rilke or rimbaud
maybe, not a man / woman & prostitute
not a [bank note/ manifestation / homosexual] etc. & etc.
(oh, the virtues of the accomplished & the self-proclaimed)
to be honest, I'm a bull shackled in an abandoned house
with no lack of creature comforts
my body porous with electric-plug bites
each day, i chew up grassy green & ten dead bodies
devour 30 kilowatts of electricity and still crave for more.
    —from "who are you"

Rather than reconstructing a burnished image of history, in this poetry we often find denials or rejections: indignation and outrage in Nguyễn Quốc Chánh's works, affliction in the form of sarcasm or empathy in Trần Tiến Dũng's poems, derision and apathy in the poetry of Phan Bá Thọ, all tinted with a shade of desperation. History is positioned on the edge of an abyss. No longer having the status of Truth, history is questioned and questions itself, it is derided and is itself a derision. It seems that when individuals look into the mirror of history, they find only their own empty image, an image completely erased by treachery, a treachery in which through collective amnesia we have almost forgotten our role as accomplices. Each successive unmasking takes the form of negating the past, playing with or making fun of the act of recounting laughable historical fictions. As if it is only by stripping history of its sacral robe that we can lay bare its artful deception and its sins, and recover our trampled and effaced image. It is easy to understand how history, in this sense, has become a substantial theme. Is this just an attempt, however, to blindly absolve and justify the burden of poetry by pointing the finger at history? Is history, as a result, shouldering burdens that are not really its own? Could we reconstitute the same set of questions, substituting "regime" for "history"?

In juxtaposition with the negation of history exists the negation of poetry itself in order to create | politicize poetry: Nguyễn Quốc Chánh strongly denies, abnegates, repudiates the very ways in which he penned his previous works, while poets like Phan Bá Thọ purposely create trash, no longer "making poetry". For many years now, Nguyễn Quốc Chánh, Trần Tiến Dũng, and Phan Bá Thọ seem to have refused to continue writing poetry or to present themselves as poets. Allow me to share my suspicions: as the poetry struggled to negate history [as it says and it does], it aspired to sacrifice itself in a massive parade. When the poetry denies, abnegates, repudiates the literary history from which it emerges, it refuses to keep treading the path set in its past: it seeks ruptures, seeks to prove that a breach has been made, and finds nihilistic amusement in becoming an endless poetic landfill.

To return to the question of dissident poetry, personally, I would like to think that this label is reserved for a distinct sector of poetry that may no longer have so many reasons to exist, as its existence could be considered a consequence of favoring political preferences at the expense of poetry or, at the same time, at the expense of politics. There should be no reason for poets to self-censor sociopolitical issues out of their works as "apoetical" matters; there should also be no reason for poets to commit to political themes just to fulfill expectations regarding the pragmatically potential power or responsibility of poetry. Hence, just as we readily concur with the need to resist uniform, propagandistic, and laudatory politics, to resist the political preference of conforming and bowing down to a monopolistic state, to fend off the illusions of an apolitical freedom, and to seek democratic exchanges, as readers we demand

Nhã Thuyên

more elaborate discussions regarding the politics of poetry, specific to each creative work in its own right, and we demand the overthrow of the monopolistic oppression and self-censorship inherent in each writer. From another point of view, the altruistic essence of aesthetics seems to be at odds with the resoluteness of ideological protest, and this is one reason why I shall not proclaim that poems that don't have an obvious dissident flavor, but instead only seem to explore the expressive dynamics of words, for instance, are any less political than poems that are reactionary, insurgent, or dissenting. Without dwelling on the conflicts between the different social functions and aesthetics of poetry, or on the possibility of reaching a balance, I consider that the power of negation in poetry, and in art as a whole, cannot merely be reduced to an antagonistic ideological voice, or even more so merely to propagandistic texts that support different opinions or sides. Poetry, in its effort to participate in common concerns and accounts of history, always arises from a need to raise one's own voice. Perhaps it's time for some ghosts to stop terrifying.

Work Cited

Bùi Chát. "Đèn đỏ." ("Red Light.") *Bài thơ một vần [Poems of a Single Rhyme]*, Sai Gon:Giấy Vụn Press, 2010. Print.

Chế Lan Viên and Vũ Thị Thường. "Ai? Tôi!" ["Who? I!"] Di Cảo Thơ. [Posthumous Poetry], Volume 3, Edited by Chế, Lan V, and Thị T. Vũ, *Di Cảo Thơ*. Huế: Nhà xuất bản Thuận Hóa, 1992. Print.

Nguyễn Minh Châu. "Hãy đọc lời ai điếu cho một giai đoạn văn học minh hoạ." ["Let's Give a Funeral Oration for an Era of Illustrative Literature."] *Trang giấy trước đèn [Pages Written by Lamplight]*, Hà Nội: Khoa học xã hội, Press, 1994.

Nguyễn Quốc Chánh. "Hậu, hậu, nhưng không phải hậu." ["Post-, Post-, But Not Really Post- ..."]. *Ê, tao đây. ["Hey, I'm here"]*. Sài Gòn, 2005. Print.

Phan Bá Thọ. "thụ cảm-october." ["Apperceive-october."] *Đống rác vô tận [Endless Landfil]*, Sài Gòn, 2004. Print.

—."mày là ai." ["Who Are You."] *Đống rác vô tận [Endless Landfil]*, Sài Gòn: samizdat, 2004. Print.

Thanh Thảo. "Bày tỏ." ["Confession."]. *Văn nghệ [Art & Letters]* Journal,   v.34, 22 Aug. 1987, www.viet-studies.info/NhaVanDoiMoi/ ThanhThao_CanDam-_VaDoanket.htm

Trần Tiến Dũng. "Chúng tôi đứng ở vỉa hè và đếm." ["We Stand on the Sidewalk and Count."]. *Mây bay là bay rồi. [The Floating Clouds Have Already Floated Away]*. Sài Gòn: samizdat, 2010. Print.

—."Cách nói của những người tử tế." ["How Nicely People Phrase It."]. *Mây bay là bay rồi. [The Floating Clouds Have Already Floated Away]*. Sài Gòn, 2010. Print.

—."Đôi chân sợ hãi, tôi chọn bước ra." ["On Trembling Feet, I Choose to Step Out."]. *Mây bay là bay rồi. [The Floating Clouds Have Already Floated Away]*. Sài Gòn. 2010. Print.

Nguyễn Quốc Chánh
translated by David Payne

Even though the pioneering poet Nguyễn Quốc Chánh has ensured his own marginalization by rejecting censorship of his work by the authorities, referring to him as "experimental" or "edgy" seems inadequate, or even unjust, when such labels have become rather meaningless in Việt Nam when applied to the merits of creative works, implying nothing more than an attitude that isn't in line with the official views on literature more-or-less imposed by state-run literary bodies, or at best a very embryonic stage of a new direction in Vietnamese poetry. It is true that there are many points in Nguyễn Quốc Chánh's life and work that enable me to reflect on how an artist can use their self as a witness, or as a piece of evidence, in order to reveal the strongly oppressive conditions of a society within which the artist is both being oppressed and striving to fight against oppression. And perhaps some readers will see such a poet as a symbol of conscience or self-sacrifice, shrouded in legend. Here, however, I do not want to exploit the case of Nguyễn Quốc Chánh as a means to examine the difficult and antagonistic relationship between an artist and the authorities, a relationship that should perhaps no longer be seen as the biggest constraint on creative expression in Việt Nam now. I don't want to see Chánh's poetry only as a way to reveal the discontent and everlasting inequality of the artist with institutions. It is true that Nguyễn Quốc Chánh has (yet) never received any recognition from mainstream arts organizations in Việt Nam, and his name may never be included on the list of writers honored by the Vietnamese Literary Associations or the nation; he himself has completely repudiated and broken away from mainstream cultural spaces, which he identifies with enslavement to official views on literature. But I want to ask: is such recognition really important for the author and his readers? The assumption that tangible "authorities" possess the power to control the freedom of the writer and the reader, the designation of what is art and the status of the artist does not lead the way to the liberation of the individual and the development of their artistic context. No, I don't want to view Nguyễn Quốc Chánh's poetry only as a symbol of transgression and protest, difficult as it may be to distinguish the literary merits of Chánh's poems from their social and political implications, as warning signals inextricably linked to the time and space in which they first appeared.

In this small essay, the essential thing that I want to do (which is also the most sincere and candid thing that I am able to do at this point) is to explore how Nguyễn Quốc Chánh's poems first encountered me, and how they remain with me, both as an imprint of his time and as a timeless expression. Honestly, the longer I spend with his words, the harder it seems to find a better path into the world of his poetry. The lingering impressions left by his collections, with their compelling themes and evolving use of language and tone over time, are just like overgrown branches that I'm taking hold of with both hands, in order to grope towards the light and to know that I haven't given up halfway.

Each of Nguyễn Quốc Chánh's poetry collections are like fragments of history, not just figuratively, but as actual unique pieces of physical evidence of the social and literary landscape that he has experienced. His first collection, *Đêm mặt trời mọc* (*Night of Rising Sun*), had only just been published in 1990, with the required number of copies submitted to the authorities in June of that year when it was recalled before it had time to reach a wide audience. Afterwards, as Nguyễn Quốc Chánh recounted: "When *Night of Rising Sun* was seized in 1990, I had been feeling that language, taking the false form of resolutions and slogans, was at risk of exhaustion and self-deception, but I stirred things up as much as possible to avoid those two outcomes." The reason that it was withdrawn and also attacked was certainly due in part to some "political" verses in which the poet expressed the state of his life and of the context in which he was living, tainted with despair and full of intimate disclosures, with a mocking, derisive tone. Published concurrently with other post-war poems in the North (that is to say, in the early 1990s), for example the works of Nguyễn Duy and Thanh Thảo, what is markedly different in the works of Nguyễn Quốc Chánh is the way he looks back at the war, not through the torment of a soldier's experience, but through measured observations, bundling up the melancholy of a shared past, a past that forms part of the much longer flow of history. Perhaps a more detailed account from Nguyễn Quốc Chánh himself will provide an explanation for this sober and melancholy attitude. In a conversation with Linh Dinh published in *Tiền Vệ* in 2005, he recounts:

> I was called up for enlistment in 1979, and I had two years standing in line in my rubber sandals and khaki helmet, occasionally firing a rifle, but fortunately I was never in battle. I think if I were in a fight it would be easy for me to become a prisoner of war, or to surrender, or to be the first one shot. I never fought in battle but I still have two scars: an ulcer in my stomach due to hunger and bad food, and an inner scar caused by unceasing pressure from a group who were constantly on edge. In those two years, I recognized that aggression is something like an instinct or a latent urge within most Vietnamese people, and this frightened me more than imaginary shootouts with Pol Pot. But fortunately, thanks to the stomach ulcer, I received an early discharge.

He defined his generation in the poem "Người cõng quá khứ" ("Piggybacking on the past"): "Our generation/Piggybacking on the past/A disabled figure from the war"; and he reflected on the time following the war: "Paper money/smelling of gunpowder/and wages/the corpses of war". The collection *Khí hậu đồ vật* (*Inanimate Weather*), which came out in 1997 after a difficult process to secure a publishing license, is an attempt to penetrate or come to terms with being trapped in the messy, complicated realm of language in order to form his own artistic view. The representation of a living space, with a cramped, suffocating, and murky atmosphere covering poems that combine words and images in unfamiliar ways to create a strange reality perhaps caused obstacles for his readers at that time, and this work remains difficult to penetrate even now.

The turning point for Nguyễn Quốc Chánh in dealing with both his own creative efforts and the surrounding literary context was marked by the publication of the e-book *Của căn cước ẩn dụ* (*Of Metaphorical Identity*) at the end of 2001 on the online forum *Talawas*. Beginning with the strong lines in the "Preamble," it is immediately clear that this collection is like a landmine detector or a bird that warns of the approaching storm: the devastating impact of the collection comes primarily not from its poetic quality, but rather from the stance of an aggrieved poet towards the State censorship mechanism of the publishing system in Việt Nam:

TN: *Viết-Lách* is a compound word, composed of the common word for "writing" (*viết*) and an archaic word which also refers to writing or marking with a pen (*lách*). The compound *Viết-Lách* has come to refer to the practice of approaching an issue indirectly, weaving or circling around a topic, to avoid being censured or criticized.

> The fear of being labeled "reactionary" quickly turned into a degrading experience. It stifled creative ability through the various artifices encoded in the phenomena known as *viết-lách*. *Lách* in the process of writing is considered clever, but in reality, it is just a kind of base cunning. It is a mindset that becomes the habit of the colonized. It is as if the Vietnamese people have completely lost the will to be human, which is the consciousness of individual freedom.
>
> —from *Của căn cước ẩn dụ* (*Of Metaphorical Identity*)

Following this e-book, Nguyễn Quốc Chánh participated in the samizdat poetry milieu in Sài Gòn, contributing to the 2005 collection *Khoan cắt bê tông* (*Cutting and Drilling Concrete*), which brought together 23 authors through the samizdat Giấy Vụn Press, and printing his personal poetry collection Ê, tao đây (*Hey, I'm Here*) in the same year. Since that collection, occasional poems, notebook entries, and personal opinions have appeared in the *Tiền Vệ* online magazine, but as of now Nguyễn Quốc Chánh has not released any further poetry collections, including the previously announced collection *Mày tiêu rồi* (*Die, Bastard*). On December, 2011, and most recently, early 2018, with "Một du kích | Guerrilla Tactics" Nguyễn Quốc Chánh held an exhibition of pottery and earthenware objects, which to my regret I have only seen through photographs.[12] I want to mention this because, for me, this endeavor and its products express a powerful conception of poetry that transcends the outward beauty of these works. At this point in time, the poet | his poetry, following the path of language, seems to have a found a place to reside, whether a safe haven or a precarious perch, whether a release from feeling or a falling into despair: that which was intended to be a sun rising in the night, a light shining in the darkness, has retreated into the darkness to rediscover itself, it has let go, pouring out like a broken pipe, and it has rejected language in favor of ideas expressed in the living shape of the earth and the fire. What shapes the destiny of a poetry collection, of poetry itself, if not the awareness of its desires and the tragedy of its existence? This consciousness reveals a strength of spirit that will not compromise with what Nguyễn Quốc Chánh refers to without compunction as "reactionary dogma;" his refusal to compromise is above all a way to assert his personal freedom, as can be seen in his inner battles, which are an expression of an ongoing process of negations within his creative activities. The negative always signifies a parallel process: destruction and cultivation, tearing down and building up, death and birth.

This conflict within Nguyễn Quốc Chánh awakened a dream that was both an ambition and also a tragedy, which can be seen as a consistent concept throughout his creative works: the dream of freedom (please permit me not to talk further about that thing called "freedom," just to preserve its abstract and meandering beauty). This overarching theme in all its various forms has, I think, its own distinct meaning in the poems of Nguyễn Quốc Chánh, because it is not just a general dream or a shared ideal, or an implicit property of the private realm of poets and poetry, and its voice is also not just expressing an author's permanent obsession with the suffocating climate and imprisoned space of society and poetry, but instead becomes the voice of shared concerns on the part of both writers and readers, and in particular by those authors burdened by the past of Việt Nam. Even more than this, it is as if the change in the poet's perception of freedom determines his whole conduct with regard to the art of writing poetry and his choice of language and tone in every phase of his life and creative work. Many years previously, in his first collection, Nguyễn Quốc Chánh had sketched out a self that was free and full of life and hope, a self that enlarged itself through being exiled and choosing to exile itself:

EN: How to free the word "freedom" from its yoking to nationalist deployment, its distortion when wrenched from utopian concept, tenet of autonomy? Here lies of pain of witnessing abstract language buck up up against its manufactured twin, when it is shelled out of possibility and open signification, siphoned into sloganeering toward ideological, confining ends. The word itself, a site of proliferative struggle.

I am the sprouting seed in the hand of the sorcerer
I am the failed harvest of the drought
I am condemned to life in the sand and dust
I am thrown into jail, smashed up in the darkness
I have forgotten myself

> Under the grinding teeth of the sun
> Under your buffeting tropical rain
> Under the gloom of repentant twilight
> I sprout and grow into me
> —from "Freedom", *Night of Rising Sun*

Like young love, "Freedom" is actually the life force of an individual or a dream, a sustaining and liberating vision. But something about that dream sends shivers down my back, not because it brings in the light, but because it reveals the path to overwhelming darkness. In the opening lines of the collection *Inanimate Weather*, Nguyễn Quốc Chánh confirms and commits himself to this concept: "The poet is an apostle always proclaiming the dream of freedom." It could be said that *Inanimate Weather* is the darkest of Nguyễn Quốc Chánh's poetic works, even though it is filled with images of the sun and of sunlight; the richness and energy of the darkness cause concurrent feelings of exhaustion and hardship, excitement, unbridled ecstasy, and destructive pain.

> In the morning facing the sun, shadows falling behind my
>   back and sunlight piercing my chest,
> At midday facing the sun, shadows pouring around my
>   feet and sunlight revolving on my hair,
> In the afternoon facing the sun, shadows falling behind
>   my back and sunlight still piercing my chest.
> —from "Untitled", *Inanimate Weather*

The dream of freedom here has become the motivation for a hopeless journey, enduring the pain of wounds inflicted by the arrows of time. Innermost secrets lie naked under the eyes of time, people, and all of existence. Or perhaps there are no longer any secrets at all? In the murky encirclement of the dense system of metaphors interwoven throughout every poem, the collection *Inanimate Weather* creates an image of a prisoner trying to escape from his own cramped body, to make an escape through his own skin, skin regularly burned by the sun, burning in the darkness, and covered in burns, to

Nhã Thuyên

escape from this frozen dead state of existence, like the cold mechanical ticking of a clock in the night. It seems as if the ecstatic versifying of his inner world, with its blend of love and physicality, the torment of memory and the illusory squalls of light/darkness, is the most enduring feeling in this collection; the dream of freedom is still attached to the dissolute personal world of a poet. But on the journey to an imaginary sea, this dream had to change: while flying over highways, and over the alleys of the city, it was caught, it was flung back, and it was unjustly beaten. Then in *Of Metaphorical Identity*, one sees how "freedom" has become like a brand on the packaging for a line of products produced in a formerly colonized country after the war. From here on, Nguyễn Quốc Chánh no longer puts forward the dream of "freedom," instead he exposes paradoxes and attempts to unmask the false freedom that he observes in the "crippled figure" of the past and the present. Although the narrative pieces in the work "Triển lãm bản địa" ("Local Exhibition"), a long monologue sequence, don't refer explicitly to "freedom," these verses slam into the body, which vomits out the hidden tragedies not of a single individual but of a sinking community, vessels thirsty for freedom sinking beneath the surface of the water, leaving only an indigenous slimy residue. Reading Segment IV, for instance, I found it hard to breathe due to the condensation and congestion of time, memory, and reality being revealed; they were all pressed together within a framework of thick, overcrowded words, like a collage, a film that makes the viewer's eyes flicker and twitch through jump cuts and images all jammed together, overlapping, fragmented, and chaotic:

Liquid pools within the hand, the artery under the heel of the palm is blocked. The blood of many decades could not reach the brain. Fugue of a bottle beating on the head. Dislocated, a company of people too late to reach the sea, at first light buried in the sand, a rising sutra. A rhapsody of felled trees. Extinguish the candles, consume the cockroach-share of the bread, an alley leads down to the river. A twisting cavern, winds from all points blowing incessantly through a drainpipe. A city that doesn't sell sex, call

142

girls spread their legs, sinking into nostalgic song. Stuffed animals, licking on the reason for their vastness. Perhaps leaden clouds, perhaps a path leading back to the fallen trees. Every morning, a face eating itself laid out on a sleepless dish, I swallow ragged breaths behind half-closed doors. Something rushed, leading nowhere. My abdomen is pinched, a 33-degree slant. It could happen at any time. Retreat on your back or go forward on your stomach. Be naked or...? And the bones will...? The sea, the fetus of the end, birds covered in oil, unable to fly away. A door ajar, a face askew. A still life of teeth, an exhibit of the whole mouth. Me alone in the corner smiling. Not breaking the silence, or knowing if it is the top or the bottom of the well. To see the comes-to-naught filling up the eternal.

—from "Local Exhibition", *Of Metaphorical Identity*

And then coming to the collection *Hey, I'm Here*, the dream of freedom only bares its flesh when various disguises are torn off, while at the same time each poem is a protest. With a blunt and challenging tone, with short, compact sentences like modern proverbs and sayings, with alliteration, Nguyễn Quốc Chánh takes advantage of certain characteristics of the Vietnamese language, full of the quality of urban life, devoid of emotion, rejecting lyricism (which had been evident in his in previous collections), and eliminating every soaring metaphor; he exposes the conditions of self-enslavement that seem to pose the greatest obstacle to "his" existence, his restlessness only seeming to make it even more of a mockery:

He has one head but up to four shadows.
He has fluid filling three-quarters of his head.
He despises his head but adores his shadow.
He hates solids and craves liquids.
He puts his head in a plastic bag.
He hangs his shadows up around the room.
He beats his head and strokes his shadow.
He's been doing the same for thirty years.

—from "Three poems", *Hey, I'm Here*

So the constant dream of freedom that is an essential, enduring factor in Nguyễn Quốc Chánh's conception of the poet was born in abstract reflection, bearing the personal nature of youth, and has at last become a series of melancholy insights into the generally inhumane living conditions of the community. Yearning for the beauty of the Buddha and Jesus has gradually been obscured by the mundane objects in the life of the individual and the society, changing from proclamation to derision, from attempts to capture the poetic beauty of metaphors to a method of creating an image of freedom—both realistic and grotesque—that is displayed in a "local exhibition." At times I was confused, wanting to distinguish between *the public poet* and *the private poet*, the one who speaks to community issues, willing to abandon the search for the poetic values of language in order to speak out with a strongly individual voice that could speak for many, and the one who only values personal matters. Previously, I viewed Nguyễn Quốc Chánh as a clear example of someone changing from a private poet to a public poet, through what was perhaps an inevitable process, as though in his successive collections his quest into the interior world of the poet was inexorably replaced by indignation and strong condemnation in response to the general problems of the society, of the Vietnamese people, and of the nation. Now, I find I was mistaken: the personal in Nguyễn Quốc Chánh has transcended the dimensions of the poet himself and has taken on the nature of a public gathering. Has not the dream of freedom of which he spoke transcended the abstract meaning of poetry? It is as if he is even ready to destroy his own ego, created by his imagination and poetic imagining, and turn it into a piece of physical evidence, a reflection of himself and of the important issues facing the community, the people, and the nation that find a strange unity in his poetry. Awareness of the destiny of the dream can become an implicit signal, an implicit structural form, submerged in each of Nguyễn Quốc Chánh's poems, an underlying element binding together concerns and observations, binding together the seemingly disconnected and chaotic phrases and images in his poems. I envision he knows clearly that abstract dreams of spiritual freedom are no longer capable of comforting and soothing the dissatisfaction he feels with the institutions of society, and there is no absolute spiritual freedom in the world of poetry; freedom needs to be recognized in its full pathetic reality, and it needs to be expressed in the form of specific demands and responses to the power that is suppressing it. He understands that freedom is a way that doesn't yet have a way, an arduous struggle, a Ulyssean voyage. He understands that freedom, before coming to pass, needs to escape from the gulag. In the fight between light and darkness, he understands that it belongs to the darkness, to the shadows of the past and of the time in which he is living, where space and time are getting colder (like the title of one of his poems). He understands that the dream of freedom may no long be a response that calls out in hope and life, but rather a reflection of desperate phantoms facing their end. Perhaps he himself recognized that the face of that freedom had been disfigured, and the body of that freedom had shrunk away from the sky and the dissolute sea, it had crept into a refuge beneath a face distorted in outrage, with darting eyes always seeing clearly the walls of the prison.

The marked change in the imagery and tone throughout his poetry collections, especially in the poems that directly expressed his protest, are another facet that shows the strange unity between the private person and the public person in Nguyễn Quốc Chánh. Each of his individual creations became at the same time a way to express his poetic attitude to the reading and writing community around him. When his work first appeared, Nguyễn Quốc Chánh must have provoked the aesthetic of mainstream poetry at that time, still burdened by socialist realism, especially in the North where writers has been attached to the singuarility of this literary theory and methodology for a long time, as seen in the paradoxical imagery of this allegory:

I was trapped under the wings of a swarm of flies
And sang out with their buzzing

I carried dead bodies in my blood
The flies took me out on their backs
    —from "Flies", *Night of Rising Sun*

Still showing his passion for redrawing human portraits, which is also a way of drawing a self-portrait, Nguyễn Quốc Chánh objectifies himself, twisting his face in all directions to observe, like a multi-faced wooden statue denied the discovery of the world of imagination and emotion:

Seen from in front: my face is shameless
Seen from the side: my face is slanted
Seen from above or below: my face is soiled"
    —from "Post-, Post-, But Not Really Post- …", *Hey, I'm Here*

In fact, this face that he twists to observe has had its meaning as a manifestation, or a substitute for the individual, an abstraction of his identity, degraded in order that it might become a symbolic face, the face of the community, or even the face of the nation. It is a tangible thing, but at the same time it is also the property of a public museum, a museum of human memories. His poetry is no longer merely a reflection of himself. The individual has been unified with history; language describing the individual intersects with language interpreting history. The body of the individual has become a self-fictionalized autobiography in material form, or it has become complicated in the same way as the surrounding social climate. From this perspective, if there is a portrait of Chánh, it could be visualized as a self-portrait that has placed itself, or has been placed, to soak in an extremely toxic solution—I don't know who it is that prepared this solution—and then, that portrait, or self-dissolution, or noxious weed springing up, becomes a litmus paper to test that same solution. I think that the reader can more or less measure the toxicity of the society in this portrait, through which he exposes himself to us through language.

The communal human emerges most powerfully when Nguyễn Quốc Chánh really pours his outrage into poetry, hurling violent words, and intoning with a muscular, tense voice; language is no longer a means for him to explore and create ideas, it becomes a tool of ideas, and he rejects/abandons the attempt to write poetry as a contemplation of language in order to find a way to optimize the performance of these language tools. The unrestrained language in the radical outlook and challenging, blasphemous tone of *Hey, I'm Here* and in some other poems not included in any collection can be read, from this perspective, as a rational strategy to use language to brainwash the consciousness of the reader, which implicitly places its hope in the direct effect of language. Eliminating metaphors and imaginations, eliminating the personal narrative voice, Nguyễn Quốc Chánh does not hesitate to use taboo words, to exploit the profane humor of colloquial speech and slang, and to use definitions and bold assertions structured like folk proverbs in order to speed language up for the city streets; everything has become fitting for an open display of blasphemies, no longer hidden behind festival masks, creating a strong voice in reaction to contemporary mainstream poetry. The irony, introspection and outrage about the status quo can be felt in the way he arranges his words to form slogans, so that "Việt Nam" becomes a dartboard, enduring attacking darts, as in the following poem:

To kill rats, nothing beats the rat-killing glue biotechnology of Việt Nam.

To kill writers, nothing beats herding them into the Literary Association of Việt Nam.

To kill students, nothing beats awarding them doctorates in Việt Nam.

To cheat gullible people, nothing beats being a spiritual leader in Việt Nam.

To play games with puppets, nothing beats being a delegate to the National Assembly of Việt Nam.

Nhã Thuyên

To play games with civilized culture, nothing beats being a citizen of the capital of Việt Nam.

To know the future, nothing beats listening to a fortune teller in Việt Nam.

To know the past, nothing beats reading the history of the Communist Party of Việt Nam.

To know where the present is leading, nothing beats driving a vehicle in the streets of Việt Nam.

To be inspired to debauchery, nothing beats feasting on dog meat on the sidewalk in Việt Nam.

To be inspired as a reactionary, nothing beats passing through customs in Việt Nam.

To be inspired to heroics, nothing beats going down into the tunnels of Việt Nam.

&

To understand the meaning of the word blandishment, nothing beats being a citizen of the Socialist Republic of Việt Nam.
—from "Blandishment", *Hey, I'm Here*

I imagine how Nguyễn Quốc Chánh injected a stimulant into his words, and I imagine these words going about the streets in their naked and distressed bodies, impassive, radical, angry, or sneering, at all times causing severe provocation. Nguyễn Quốc Chánh's dense urban language doesn't seem to be just a tactic or technique, but instead reveals the flesh-and-blood relationship of the poet with the city (Sài Gòn) where he has mostly lived and within which he seems to have immersed himself. A fair relationship, expressed in the way he treats the city, both tender and detached: tender when he buries himself in the language of the streets, and detached when he observes

148

it. Nguyễn Quốc Chánh owes no birthplace debt to Sài Gòn, a city rapidly modernizing but at the same time bearing a heavy heritage of the past or of a mythical past. He seems to have never expressed a sense of nostalgia for the city's past like that expressed by outstanding poets of his age such as Trần Tiến Dũng and Nguyễn Quang Thiều. He is like a wild wolf in the city, but not lost or uncertain about where he resides. He brought the wild dark ego of the rivers of Bạc Liêu into the city of Sài Gòn to test his tensile strength as a piece of evidence/a witness. No nostalgia, no attachment, and no recollection of his roots. His identity, if he has one, lies in his collision with those spaces in which he lives. Of course, this collision is also stressful: not infrequently the urban space oppresses his body, coerces his thoughts and torments his poetry, and he constantly has to release this pressure by intense strain of reason.

Chánh's poems relay life from the rebellious graffiti-covered walls, conveying the unflinching defiance or reckless audacity of city-dwellers to defend themselves in life. The poem "Đụ vỡ sọ" ("Fuck Until the Head Explodes"), printed in the collection *Drilling and Cutting Concrete*, can be read like a Party traitor's slogan sprayed on the walls of the city in the workers' residential areas. The poem leads the reader through intense interrogations about the words which he claims are the most beautiful (though rarely written) in Vietnamese: Cunt, Cock, and Fuck, asserting that "after 10 centuries of stewing by the Chinese, Cunt, Cock and Fuck have taken on other colors: Vagina, Penis and Intercourse." With language that is both severe and humorous, the language of a guy ready to sink into the mud and to scour life's pavements, and at the same time full of imagination and personal experiences, Nguyễn Quốc Chánh has recreated a history of these

TN: *Khoan cắt bê tông (Cutting and Drilling Concrete)* is a typical phrase painted on walls in Vietnamese cities to advertise the service of cutting and drilling concrete, however the word for drilling (*khoan*) can also imply "to Fuck".

suppressed words; he prizes them from the gutter, exposes them to the light, and returns to them their former crowns that had been taken away by fear and human slavery. I see here a rare brilliance in the way he uses these forbidden words, provocative in both their sound and meaning, egalitarian ways of naming things, verses that don't call for overthrow, which are themselves full of the power to overthrow. Please read one passage from *Khoan cắt bê tông* (*Cutting and Drilling Concrete*):

> If Jesus didn't ask: If there is anyone among you who has not yet fucked, let him first cast a stone at her?! (Their shame saved Mary Magdalene from the hail of stones). Why doesn't your shame make you give equality back to Cunt, Dick and Fuck? When I close my eyes (unifying my soul and body), I see them as stars, or avatars, with the energy of great emotion and mystical activity. Cunt is the distant echo of the drum, the bell and primitive memory. [...] And when I pronounce 'Cunt', I hear its resounding echo from ancient tombstones, from the immense compassion of the Buddha and from the infinite uncertainty of memory. Over the past 10 years, I have been thrown over three times, and my former wife married another man. I became a guy who only Fucks the sand. I don't know how many times I lay down, prostrating myself on the sand, tenderly watching the sunrise through half-closed eyes. As I watched I saw a shift from red to black. It was no longer a sparkling red aureole; it turned into a shimmering and obsessive black hole. The blood in my body began to race and the red blood cells rushed down to my navel. My Cock was warm and hard. My Cock swelled up. My Cock exulted. My hands dug into the sand, my stomach pressed down into the sand, my mouth gaped open as the sand and my ass rotated.

From these stories about suppressed words, concepts like "time" and "history"—typically represented as huge, lurking, obscure phantoms—become specific and clear. The word game of the poet is about recovering suppressed ideas, a game in which the participants have to wallow in the black mud of the

150

past and present, both submerged and struggling to free themselves. Through confrontation and creating a confrontational will, casting aside power and resisting any timidity in his use of language, Nguyễn Quốc Chánh overcomes and challenges social taboos in contemporary Vietnamese life. The underlying factor in Nguyễn Quốc Chánh's creative activities and works, giving them a value that transcends the hysteria of poetry and of poets in expressing concern and venting outrage about the state of society, lies, I think, in the unity of his poetic art and the degree to which it reflects a commitment both to the present and to the history of the writer, creating a compelling and tragic beauty in his poetry.

The poetic nature and potential impact of Nguyễn Quốc Chánh's creative activities and the resulting products should probably be regarded as an unanswered question. What is the source of Nguyễn Quốc Chánh's appeal? His attitude to poetry? His stance of political opposition? The way he poses questions? His ever-changing language, twisting like a gecko's body, which can be imagined as a caricature of the struggle between light and darkness within the poet himself? His intense poetic voice, like a gushing broken drain, as deafening as a hammer and as piercing as the rhythms of the city? Above all, I want to see in his work a poet fusing his private and public selves, a poet strongly committed to the power and critical value of poetry and social engagement. This is just one person's perspective, looking from afar: connecting the different works, I sense the multifaceted figure of "the dream of freedom," whether manifest in words or hidden in the structure of imagery and themes, but always connected with an attempt at social criticism, even though, as I previously analyzed, the change in Nguyễn Quốc Chánh's awareness over time seems to determine his conduct in relation to the art of poetry. The most appealing aspect of Nguyễn Quốc Chánh's poetry is his strength of will, even though coming into contact with his works also creates a sense of impasse on all sides, which I think reflects his own impasse when he collides with society. Putting this into the context of life and poetry in Việt Nam, immersing it in the so-called thirst for freedom, like a map on an explorer's vessel lost at the bottom of the ocean, can be read as a long tale of the road of an artist, of a poet, and of poetry itself. As a superficial sketch of the portrait of a poet who carries within himself a dream of freedom which overflows the narrow limits of a single individual, who is violently thrashing about in the awareness of being surrounded on all sides, Prometheus exposing his chest for the preening crows (crows not outside of the creative needs of the artist himself), who failed in his attempt to free himself, who speaks with the voice of the community, who brings himself as a witness, as evidence, who inhales the dark flow of the era and exhales full of outrage, and so on of course this will not be enough to recognize the portrait of Nguyễn Quốc Chánh, but I think it might be one way to visualize the role an artist who has attached his fate to the concerns about the fate of Vietnamese history in many decades past. Poetry, in certain respects, is like a heart that the poet has plucked from his chest as an offering, out of his deep faith in the survival of freedom, a self-exposed and self-destructive offering, and when we look at the poet, we see only a hollow chest and a pale face full of darkness.

For me what endures, overcoming the rise and fall of a poet's value as set by society, is how their mode of writing remains with the reader. Until now, Nguyễn Quốc Chánh's renown has not, fortunately, been accompanied by widespread acclamation, and he perhaps remains an isolated and challenging figure. At one time I just saw Nguyễn Quốc Chánh as a symbol of the conscience of Vietnamese poetry in a period of crisis in writers' attitudes. But I now think I was mistaken: viewing him as a symbol turns our thoughts into clichés. Truly, who is Nguyễn Quốc Chánh to me personally? He is still a dark sculpture that is not easy to discover, his poetic works trapped in thick tangled roots. Even now, I still feel moved whenever I open the pages of old books or open websites to read his work not as a symbol of suffering and resistance, but as a poet always seeking some way to overcome personal limitations in order to explore the fresh potential of poetry and of alternative spaces for poetry. I think, even, the way a poet's works stay with the reader can overcome those things that the poet believes over time, and can overcome all of the failures they may feel in relation to poetry, in the face of the exhaustion of language and their own fundamental need to write poetry. Through his actions, poetry, and everything else, Nguyễn Quốc Chánh is a presence of violation, of resistance, of refusal and, that means, of creativity. In one poem, Nguyễn Quốc Chánh describes the plight of birds throwing themselves into a stone crevasse and dying, a mass suicide with all their beaks pecking each other, a syndrome of traumas in their flesh. I see in it the image of poets bearing within themselves the violent explosions of memory, and the multiple deaths that reside within profoundly painful lines of poetry:

Syndrome

Birds pass through the slit one by one.
They:
One by one wings disappear.
One by one songs are stilled.
One by one only beaks remain.
One by one pecking each other's eyes and necks,

They do not see death lurking in the curved branches.
They do not see the forest of guns growing in each eye socket of the land.

They only hear the sound of weapons concealed under slabs of fat.
They only hear the sound of a gun being loaded, deep inside the brain.

Nhã Thuyên

Work Cited

Linh Dinh. "Nói chuyện với Nguyễn Quốc Chánh" ["Speaking with Nguyễn Quốc Chánh"], *Tiền Vệ*, Web. 2005. www.tienve.org/home/literature/viewLiterature.do?action=viewArtwork&artworkId=37

Nguyễn Quốc Chánh. "Xuống đường" [Down the Road], *Tiền Vệ*. Web. 2005. http://tienve.org/home/literature/viewLiterature.do?action=viewArtwork&artworkId=12075

—."Người cõng quá khứ." [Piggybacking on the past.], *Đêm Mặt Trời Mọc: Thơ. Thành phố^ [Night of the Rising Sun]*. Sài Gòn: Trẻ, 1990. Print.

—."Lời nói đầu" ["Preamble"], *Của căn cước ẩn dụ. [Of Metaphorical Identity.]*, *Talawas*, Web. 2001. www.talawas.org/talaDB/showFile.php?res=922&rb=0101

—."Tự do" ["Freedom"], *Đêm Mặt Trời Mọc: Thơ. Thành phố^ [Night of the Rising Sun]*. Sài Gòn: Trẻ, 1990. Print.

—. "Không đề." ["Untitled."], *Inanimate Weather [Khí hậu đồ vật]*. Sài Gòn: Trẻ, 1997. Print.

—. "Triển lãm bản địa." ["Local Exhibition."], Của căn cước ẩn dụ. [Of Metaphorical Identity.] Ebook, *Talawas*, 2001.

—. "Ba bài thơ." ["Three Poems."] *Ê, tao đây. [Hey, I'm here.]*. Sài Gòn, 2005. Print

—. "Ruồi" ("Flies"), *Đêm Mặt Trời Mọc: Thơ. Thành phố^ [Night of the Rising Sun]*. Sài Gòn: Trẻ, 1990. Print.

—. "Hậu, hậu, nhưng không phải hậu." ["Post-, Post-, But Not Really Post- ..."]. *Ê, tao đây. [Hey, I'm Here]*. Sài Gòn, 2005. Print.

—. "Phỉnh" ("Blandishment"), Ê, tao đây. [Hey, I'm Here]. Sài Gòn, 2005. Print.

—."Đụ vỡ sọ" ["Fuck Until the Head Explodes"], *Khoan cắt bê tông (Cutting and Drilling Concrete)*, Sài Gòn: Giấy Vụn Press, 2005. Print

—. "Hội chứng" ["Syndrome"], *Của căn cước ẩn dụ. [Of Metaphorical Identity.]* Ebook, Talawas, 2001.

154

Afterwords:
Thinking Together, Thinking Forward,
Thinking Differently with Nhã Thuyên

Afterwords:
Thinking Together, Thinking Forward,
Thinking Differently with Nhã Thuyên
written by Trần Ngọc Hiếu
translated by Nguyễn Hoàng Quyên

Any human power can be resisted and changed by
human beings. Resistance and change often begin in
art, and very often in our art, the art of words.

— Ursula K. Le Guin

1. The title of this essay collection consists of word
combinations that are unusual, almost unprecedented
in the Vietnamese language. The word play already
present in the book's title is not simply a rhetorical device
deployed by Nhã Thuyên to poeticize the language of
the essay form. Nhã Thuyên carries a need to invent
ways of articulation that might initially sound jarring
or indulgent when expressing her meditations on the
underground movements of Việt Nam's contemporary
literary scene, and to a larger extent, of Việt Nam's
current social sphere. She wishes to avoid regions of
ready-made vocabularies and established lingoes when
describing these movements since readily available
expressions might not prove to be compatible with
her personal experience as she observes and grasps
them. What Nhã Thuyên emphasizes right from the
opening lines of the essay collection is the dialogue
and monologue of her personal perspective, judgment,
and premonition. Persistence is the first merit that
deserves acknowledgement in this book: the author
is conscious of her participatory responsibility as she
intervenes poetry from below, from the margins of
society, while simultaneously self-positioning in a vital
distance from her subject; the pages thus appear with
avid sincerity and calm frankness, if not stark fairness.

2. The choice to sustain one's personal viewpoint invariably calls for courage, especially in Việt Nam's social context where the freedom of expression still faces various challenges. The author of this essay collection humbly articulates her spectrum of perspective: since she does not ambitiously attempt to survey the entire landscape and listen to every resonance, through a personal lens, what is presented here resembles an impressionist vignette of a reality (among many realities) that still calls for a multitude of more diverse approaches. The book is Nhã Thuyên's minor narrative on Việt Nam's poetry and society of the now. And it is with this approach through the prism of minor narrative that this collection manages to notice the shifts, cracks, and incipient seeds profoundly eclipsed in reality. The book therefore is capable of provoking multiple representations of Việt Nam's literature and society that have previously been narrowly framed.

What is Vietnamese literature? In this book, Nhã Thuyên shows the necessity of understanding this concept in its pluralism. The emergence of the Internet has deterritorialized the definition of ethnic literature framed within geographic borders and blurred the distinction between "local literature" and "diasporic literature" in order to form a perhaps more capacious concept—"Vietnamese-language literature." But "Vietnamese-language literature," through what we learn from this essay collection, should be understood as multilingual entity in which multiple voices resonate and multiple Vietnamese existences carry different memories and histories.

Another observation by Nhã Thuyên that reveals the need to view "Vietnamese literature" as a pluralistic entity is the marginalized presences which have so far been unidentified in the accounts of literary history being introduced in lecture halls across Vietnamese universities. The marginalized here is the space of minor voices, convention-breaking choices, or to borrow Nhã Thuyên's expression, "[self-]vanishing presences." They are the voices of feminine beings in poetry, digital samizdat phenomena, or a presence almost too taboo for mainstream poetry criticism— Nguyễn Quốc Chánh. Looking at these peripheries, the essay collection envisions a present Việt Nam very differently from clichéd representations of Việt Nam as a country of war, a nation ruled by a hegemonic ideology, an exotic touristic location, and so forth. Contemporary Việt Nam, from Nhã Thuyên's personal point of view, necessitates an imagination that is livelier, more complex, and less prejudiced: a Việt Nam with its own tales which double as shared stories about the freedom of expression and the struggle to locate a voice by humans in many places in the world, such as the story of feminism or youth culture. Poetry, for Nhã Thuyên, would offer a space of possibilities for voices that must be uttered and heard, especially if "cultural dialogism" that opens space for multiple voices—to borrow a Mikhail Bakhtin's term—were truly respected.

3. Poetry has too often been made to accept the status of the marginalized. During the times of Plato, the poet was already a thorn in the eyes of the philosopher who wanted to design an ideal republic. In the Romantic period when poetry seemingly enjoyed a significant role in the cultural sphere, poets were still merely defined as "the unacknowledged legislators of the world" (Percy Bysshe Shelley). The peripheral poets whom Nhã Thuyên reads are perhaps compatible with George Oppen's idea of the role of the poet: "Poets are the legislators of the unacknowledged world." In this essay collection, many voices speak of their conditions: there are many worlds of voices forcefully suppressed by grand narratives. Poetry, then, seems to be the only way to utter, the very thing on which the peripheral

ones could trustingly lean and stand, to borrow an idea of Phùng Quán: "Có những phút ngã lòng/ Tôi vịn câu thơ mà đứng dậy" "The moments my heart falls/ I lean on the poetry to stand up". (A parenthetical note of Phùng Quán (1932-1995) might make more sense here: as a participant of the Nhân Văn–Giai Phẩm affair, Phùng Quán was disciplined and sent to rehabilitation camps for many years. Later, he along with multiple artists and writers involved in this movement were banned from their practice for almost half a century. In 2007, Phùng Quán was awarded the Vietnamese government's State Prize for the Arts and Letters, which was signed by the President of Việt Nam and also awarded to Trần Dần, Lê Đạt, and Hoàng Cầm. Phùng Quán's poetry—something that remains intimate and essential to his life—then has been republished.)

Nhã Thuyên's essay collection, most of all, has displayed a dishevelled crime scene created by the marginal pulse of poetry in the first decade of the 21st century when Vietnam's cultural landscape underwent significant shifts, the most major consequence of which was the decentering trend that unfolded across multiple life dimensions—something Nhã Thuyên acknowledges as an opportunity rather a loss. The energy of marginal poetry focuses on acts that could be gathered in the form of words associated with

Sáng Tạo (The Creation) group consisted of writers and artists who were students from North Việt Nam and migrated to the South in the early 1950s. They founded Creation magazine, which turned into a movement for literary emancipation in the South. After 1975, under the Democratic Republic regime, the authors, and works of the Creation group, together with the South's literary heritage, became a lost legacy.

the ecstatic state of revolution: "provocative," "revolt," "resistance," "refusal," and so on. To speak more imag- istically, to reuse a poetic idea by Linh Dinh, this arduous process of "giải phẫu vành tai tiếng Việt | reha- bilitating the Viet- namese auricle" is fundamentally an effort to negate all rules, canons, and assumptions for- merly accepted in poetry. Following what Nhã Thuyên

> Thơ Mới (New Poetry) is considered the first modern poetry movement in Việt Nam. Established in the early 1930s, under the influence of Western literature, most explicitly French literature, New Poetry severed itself from the classical poetry tradition influenced by China to enter the orbit of Western Romanticism.

unveils in this essay collection, it is absolutely sensible to say, never since Thơ Mới (the New Poetry) movement in the early 1930s, besides the late-1950s manifestos and renewals by Sáng Tạo (The Creation) group in the South and the muted explorations of Nhân Văn—Giai Phẩm poets who had to wait nearly forty years for a formal reintroduction, has there been such a raging tempest in the Vietnamese poetic realm. Trash spilled into poetry, the vulgar filled the poetic, meaninglessness became where poetry wanted to arrive. Jokes, jests, and blas- phemies became legitimate ways of uttering poetry.

It could be considered fortunate, or not, depending on the point of view, when this tempest, as with all tempests, eventually died down. But the scene of the crime and the damage done by such a tempest remained unmeasured | unmeasurable for the majority of Viet- namese mainstream literary critics during the decade that followed. To describe this tempest would be to warn about a potential destabilization of what has been most stalwart, powerful, and perpetuated by taboos or laws.

To expose it would be synonymous with an acknowl-
edgment that poetry might *not* be what people would
like to label, name, or turn into conventions, and fur-
ther, an acceptance that poetry is always more *free* than
common assumptions. And to mention it would mean to
discern other possibilities of growth in places uprooted
by the tempest and to notice the births blooming upon the
ground of devastation. The tempestuous energy turns
out to not become exhausted but partly transformed
into many indie I underground cultural phenomena still
emerging and spreading across present-day Vietnam.

4. The inquiries and viewpoints Nhã Thuyên shares
    in this book are significant academic questions
    when researching movements of early 21st century
    Vietnamese literature and society even though the
    author has chosen to write in a way that maximally
    blurs the academic aspect and accentuates personal
    experience. But it is certainly possible to notice
    questions that should be discussed more thoroughly
    from Nhã Thuyên's discoveries. For example, the
    relationship between public spheres and the arts in
    modern Vietnamese history is still an open question
    to be probed further. Another research question that
    promises a multitude of challenging opinions might
    be a comparative view on continuity and discontinu-
    ity between the marginal poetic practices described
    in this collection and the revolutions or revolutionary
    ambitions of modern poetic movements such as New
    Poetry, Creation, Nhân Văn–Giai Phẩm, and other
    controversial occurrences in the late 20th century.
    Furthermore, it is possible to connect these marginal
    poetic phenomena to poetic practices closely associated
    with popular culture, which are unseparated from the
    demands for democracy and free expression all over the
    world, in order to see that poetry, despite its attach-
    ments to different traditions of language and culture,
    faces shared challenges and that the poets are still

struggling in defense of "unacknowledged worlds"—a labor that demands of them the spirit of Don Quixote. This essay collection could also be suitably added to the history of samizdat—a cultural phenomenon that turns out to be no mere heritage of the past in Việt Nam and the world. The most reassuring promise of this book is the invitation to think forward and think differently from what the author has portrayed. In this sense, the essay collection bears an admirable spirit of democracy.

5. The process of shaping this essay collection is in itself a narrative worthy of retelling though Nhã Thuyên barely mentioned the extremely severe trials she endured to defend her personal view. Perhaps the author herself would prefer me not to reiterate what she has suffered during the past six years of pursuing this project, which started as a research question at her university, where she first received the onslaught of crackdowns on academic freedom. But "un\ \martyred" is not only a spiritual feature inscribed in the poetic phenomena Nhã Thuyên observed but her own attitude as she deals with the unceasing aftermath. The book does not satisfy readers who anticipate a literary scandal, it resists reducing or exploiting the image of the author as an icon of dissidence. Nhã Thuyên refuses to become a representative voice for anyone: despite its coverage of poetic phenomena that were once challenging and provocative, the entire book turns out to be a voice that is low, soft, composed and yet absolutely genuine and courageous. I could feel the patience of Nhã Thuyên's phrasing labor as she strives to maintain such a tone and rhythm throughout the book.

After all, literature does not necessarily have to bear witness to histories; it manifests individual existences through their singular voices. How far would Nhã Thuyên's resonant voice reach, and what responses might this essay collection receive? I perhaps ought not to make proclamations here. But as long as such a voice remains utterable, it means even the most maddening noise would not manage to drown out a free individual. Free beings often are uncompromising, reject external expectation and act in accordance with urgencies from within. Such beings might be difficult for us to instantly embrace but with more patient listening, we see that only those beings could tell different stories about the world–like the stories about Việt Nam which I believe will surprise many readers of this book: a deeply intimate Việt Nam of Nhã Thuyên, a Việt Nam more capacious than geographical demarcations, a Việt Nam seen from "anti-poetics," a Việt Nam of restlessness and desire, of frustration and breakage. And yet, here is a Việt Nam where internal present movements echo the conscious rhythms of parallel beings at large.

Walls Speak

A collage of words cut from the working manuscript and nonsense drawings by
Nhã Thuyên and Yên San on a (photo of) wall in Hà Nội.

Wall photograph by Nhã Thuyên. A0 Paper, December 2018.

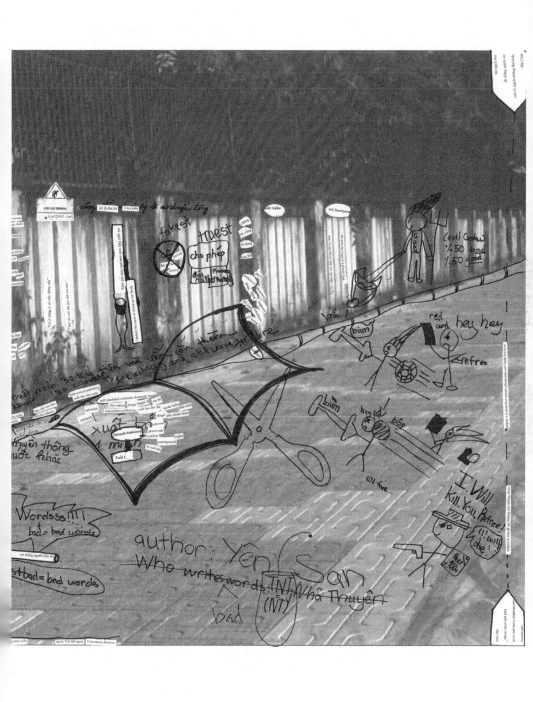

Endnotes:

1. Václav Havel was introduced in Vietnamese with the translation of the essay "The Power of the Powerless – Quyền lực của không quyền lực" by Khải Minh, Talawas 2006. Archived at: http://www.talawas.org/talaDB/showFile.php?res=6321&rb=08. The whole book, *The Power of the Powerless – Quyền lực của không quyền lực*, then published exclusively with the permission of Václav Havel given to the Giấy Vụn publisher, Vietnamese translation by Phạm Nguyên Trường (2013).

2. Đỗ Mười - *Báo chí Văn Nghệ trong sự nghiệp Đổi Mới* [*The Literary and Arts Media in the Cause of Renovation*] – Sự Thật (Truth) Publishing House, Hà Nội, 1989.

3. Phạm Thị Hoài – *Nhà văn thời Hậu Đổi Mới* [A Post-Renovation Writer], *Talawas* 10.2.2004. Archived at: http://www.talawas.org/talaDB/showFile.php?rb=0401&res=411.

4. Worth mentioning are "Hai ngày đáng ghi nhớ mãi" ["Two Unforgettable Days"] in Văn Nghệ (Arts and Letters) on the 17th of October 1987–Record of the two-day meeting of Secretary-General Nguyễn Văn Linh with around 100 writers and artists on 6 and 7 October 1987, "Đồng chí Tổng bí thư Nguyễn Văn Linh nói chuyện với văn nghệ sĩ" ("Comrade Secretary-General Nguyễn Văn Linh Speaks with Writers and Artists"–Văn Nghệ (Arts and Letters), 17-10-1987), Hồ Ngọc: "Cần giải quyết đúng đắn mối quan hệ giữa văn nghệ và chính trị" ("The Need for Correct Solutions to the Relationship Between Arts and Letters and Politics"–Văn Nghệ (Arts and Letters), 21-11-1987), Nguyễn Quang Sáng: "Những điều cần cho văn học" ("Pressing Issues for Literature"), Nguyên Ngọc: "Cần phát huy đầy đủ chức năng xã hội của văn học nghệ thuật" ("The Need to Bring into Play the Social Function of Literature and Art"–Văn Nghệ (Arts and Letters) 31-10-1987), Nguyễn Hồng Phong: "Để văn nghệ ta có được nhiều đỉnh cao và phong phú" ("For Our Arts and Letters to Have Abundant Peaks and Richness" – Văn Nghệ (Arts and Letters) 5-12-1887) – cited in the volume of Lại Nguyên Ân and Nguyễn Thị Bình (collated and edited): *Đời sống văn nghệ thời đầu Đổi Mới* (Literary and Artistic Life in the Early Renovation Period), unpublished. Documents supplied by the researcher Nguyễn Thị Bình.

5. To read further: "*TIEN VE* and Freedom of Thought & Expression for Contemporary Vietnamese Arts" by Hoàng Ngọc-Tuấn (one of *Tiền Vệ* founders), *Tiền Vệ*. Archived at: https://www.

tienve.org/home/literature/viewLiterature.do?action=viewArt-
work&artworkId=8543; *"Da Màu*: một chặng đường," (*"Da
Màu*: a Journey") by Phùng Nguyên, *Da Màu*, 2010, archived at
http://damau.org/archives/17410

6. Interview with Phạm Xuân Nguyên, *Nghĩ sao nói vậy* (Plain
   Speaking), *Talawas* 21.4.2005. Accessed at: http://www.tala-
   was.org/talaDB/showFile.php?res=4337&rb=0202. Archived in
   Talawas (2005, Vietnamese only).

7. Relevant articles include "Vietnam's rude poetry delights intel-
   ligentsia" (Nga Phạm, 2004), "Letter from Hồ Chí Minh City:
   Poetry without borders" (Jean-Claude Pomonti, 2006), "Open
   Mouth & Hip Hop" (Khánh Hảo, 2005) and "Open Mouth [Mo
   Mieng]: Begins a new history in Vietnamese Literature" (Đỗ Lê
   Anhdao, 2005).

8. See articles by Trần Ngọc Hiếu: "The rebellion of the word in
   contemporary poetry, perceived through several phenomena"
   (2005), originally a submission to the conference "Literature
   after 1975, issues in research and pedagogy" at the Philology
   Department of Hà Nội National University of Education, "A
   contribution to identify young poets in the new millennium"
   (2005), "The poet and the reader in literary life today" (2005),
   "Additional commentaries on a new poetry genre" (under the
   pen name An Vân) (2005), "How to define poetry-writing: On
   contemporary poetic practices as acts of writing" (2008), a sub-
   mission to the conference "Vietnamese contemporary poetry"
   at Ho Chi Minh City University of Social Sciences and Hu-
   manities, and most recently, "Play as a disposition in Vietnam-
   ese contemporary poetry" in the essay anthology *Edges of literary
   history* which came out of the research project *Understanding Viet-
   nam* (2016). In 2012, Trần Ngọc Hiếu submitted successfully
   his doctoral thesis "Lý thuyết trò chơi và một số hiện tượng thơ
   Việt Nam đương đại | Theories of Play and Contemporary Viet-
   namese Poetry" at Hà Nội University of Education in which he
   discussed Open Mouth's poetry from a theoretical perspective
   of play.

9. See essays and articles by Đoàn Cầm Thi: "On *Concrete Cut-
   ting and Drilling*" (2005), "Again, *Concrete Cutting and Drilling*"
   (2005), "Solidarity, solidarity, great solidarity" (2006), "A new
   Vietnamese poetry: The emergence of a new poetic genre in Sài
   Gòn" (2006), originally a presentation at the seminar "D'une
   histoire des Etats-nations à une histoire des identités plurielles
   au Vietnam, Laos et Cambodge contemporains" (Paris, 2006),

"'I, an ignominious citizen, an alcoholic genie' – Poetry and Marginality in contemporary Vietnam" (2007) translated into Vietnamese on Tiền Vệ from the French original "«Moi, citoyen ignominieux, génie alcoolique...» — Poésie et marginalité dans le Vietnam contemporain" on *La Revue des Ressources* (2007).

10. See articles by Như Huy: "Few digressions on the poem 'Champion' by Bùi Chát" (2004) and "Several opinions regarding the Open Mouth group" (2005) written on the occasion of Open Mouth's cancelled reading at the Goethe Institute in Hà Nội.

11. See articles by Phan Nhiên Hạo: "Young Poets Are Not Necessarily A 'Rotten Breeze'" (2003), "Postwar Writers and the Pantless Emperor" (2004), "The New and Old in Poetry and Postmodernism" (2004), "Three (Oral) Portions" (2004), and "A Dialogue with Đoàn Cầm Thi on... Trash" (2006).

12. An introduction and some of the objects from this exhibition can be seen on the *Tiền Vệ* at: http://tienve.org/home/activities/viewActivities.do?action=viewnews&newsId=224

About the author and the companions:

Nhã Thuyên's most recent poetry thing *words breathe, creatures of elsewhere* (từ thở, những người lạ) was published in Vietnamese (Nhã Nam, 2015) and in English translation by Kaitlin Rees (Vagabond Press, 2016). With Kaitlin Rees, she found *AJAR*, a small bilingual literary journal-press, an online, printed space for poetic exchange. She soliloquies some nonsense when having no other emergencies of life to deal with.

Ngân Nguyễn lives and works in Hà Nội.

Nguyễn-Hoàng Quyên is a(n up)rooted writer-translator. After her studies at Stanford University, she works and plays with multitudes of art collectives in Hà Nội and Sài Gòn. With *AJAR* journal-press, she is fated to translate at the breathing edges of the Vietnamese language and co-host expanded poetry festivals across whispered and loud spaces.

Kaitlin Rees writes translations between Hà Nội and New York City. Born early in the morning, the year of the buffalo, she is perfectly suited to endure long suffering works, which is only one reason to fall in love with Nhã Thuyên.

Trần Ngọc Hiếu has worked as a lecturer in Hà Nội National University of Education since 2001. He earned Phds Degree in Literary Theory in 2012. His research interests include literary theories, contemporary arts and Vietnamese modern literature. Articles and essays are published in literary and several national other magazines such as *Nghiên cứu văn học* (*Literary Studies Journal*), *Văn học nước ngoài* (*Foreign Literature*), *Tạp chí Văn hóa nghệ thuật* (*Culture and Arts Journal*). He also works as a translator who has done the translations of some theoretical writings. Recently, his paper on ecocriticism (co-author with Đặng Thị Thái Hà) has appeared in Southeast Asian Ecocriticism: Theories, Practices, Prospects (edited by John Charles Ryan), Lexington Book, 2018.

David Payne lives in Hà Nội, Việt Nam and divides his time between translation of Vietnamese prose and poetry, and civil society, public health and climate change projects. His translations and original writing have appeared in *Asymptote Journal*, *White Horses* magazine in Australia, the Mekong Review, and in collections by AJAR Press. He is currently translating a novel by Trần Dần, supported in part by a grant from the Henry Luce Foundation and the Translation Project Group/AAS Southeast Asia Council.

Roof Books
the best in language since 1976

Recent & Selected Titles

THE RESIGNATION by Lonely Christopher, 104 p. $16.95
POLITICAL SUBJECT by Caleb Beckwith, 112 p. $17.95
ECHOLOCATION by Evelyn Reilly, 144 p. $17.95
HOW TO FLIT by Mark Johnson. 104 p. $16.95
(((...))) by Maxwell Owen Clark. 136 p. $16.95
The Reciprocal Translation Project
edited by Sun Dong & James Sherry. 208 p $22.95
DETROIT DETROIT by Anna Vitale. 108 p. $16.95
Goodnight, Marie, May GodHave Mercy on Your Soul
by Marie Buck. 108 p. $16.95
BOOK ABT FANTASY by Chris Sylvester. 104 p. $16.95
NOISE IN THE FACE OF by David Buuck. 104 p. $16.95
PARSIVAL by Steve McCaffery. 88 p. $15.95
dead letter by Jocelyn Saidenberg. 94 p. $15.95
social patience by David Brazil. 136 p. $15.95
The Photographer by Ariel Goldberg. 84 p. $15.95
TOP 40 by Brandon Brown. 138 p. $15.95
THE MEDEAD by Fiona Templeton. 314 p. $19.95
LYRIC SEXOLOGY VOL. 1 by Trish Salah. 138 p. $15.95
INSTANT CLASSIC by erica kaufman 90 p. $14.95
Motes by Craig Dworkin. 88 p. $14.95
Both Poems by Anne Tardos. 112 p. $14.95

Roof Books are published by
Segue Foundation
300 Bowery • New York, NY 10012
For a complete list, please visit *roofbooks.com*

Roof Books are distributed by
SMALL PRESS DISTRIBUTION
1341 Seventh Street • Berkeley, CA. 94710-1403
spdbooks.org